MACBETH

ENJOY SHAKESPEARE

King Lear
Macbeth
Much Ado About Nothing
Romeo and Juliet
Twelfth Night

Check for coming titles at www.FullMeasurePress.com

ENJOY SHAKESPEARE

Macbeth

By

William Shakespeare

A Verse Translation

By

Kent Richmond

 Full Measure Press • Lakewood, California

Published by
Full Measure Press
P.O. Box 6294
Lakewood, Calif. 90714-6294 USA

For ordering information visit www.FullMeasurePress.com

Library of Congress Control Number: 2006933191

ISBN-13, print ed.   978-0-9752743-8-5
ISBN-10, print ed.   0-9752743-8-4

First Printing

Printed in the United States of America

Contents

Illustrations

Front matter illustration and illustration on page 159 from *Galerie des Personage de Shakspeare* (1844), compiled by Amédée Pichot (1795-1877). Paris: Baudry, Librairie Européenne.

Illustrations on pages 15, 48, 81, 87, and 142 from *The Works of Shakespeare, Vol. 1* (1877), edited by Howard Staunton; illustrations by Sir John Gilbert, R.A. (1817-1897)/engraved by the Brothers Dalziel. London: George Routledge and Sons.

Illustrations on pages 61 and 69 from *Shakespeare in Pictorial Art* (1916) by Malcolm C. Salaman (text) and Charles Holme (ed.). London: "The Studio" Ltd. Page 61, detail from "Lady Macbeth" by George Cattermole (1800-1868); page 69, detail from "Macbeth Instructing the Murderers" also by George Cattermole.

Illustrations on pages 39 and 132 from *The Royal Shakespeare* (1894). London, Paris, and Melbourne: Cassell and Company Limited. Page 39, from "Macbeth and Lady Macbeth" by V. W. Bromley (1848-1877); page 113, "Macbeth and Macduff" by A. Fredericks.

Illustration on page 113 from *Cassell's Illustrated Shakespeare* (1915) New York and London: Funk & Wagnalls Co. "Miss Violet Vanbrugh as Lady Macbeth" from a painting by Charles Buchel (1872-1950).

About this Translation

This translation makes the language of William Shakespeare's drama more contemporary without modernizing the play in any other way. No lines are omitted or simplified, and no characters or scenes are deleted.

My aim is for readers to experience Shakespeare's plays with the level of challenge and comprehension offered to audiences 400 years ago. Despite the richness of the plays, theatergoers in that era did not need scene summaries to follow the plot, footnotes to interpret vocabulary, or elaborate gestures to help them recognize a joke or guess at a character's intentions or emotional state. After all, Shakespeare's characters tell us what they are thinking. The plays lasted only a couple of hours, which means the actors spoke at a fairly rapid, though comfortable, pace.

To qualify this translation as authentic Shakespeare, I preserve the metrical rhythm of the original as much as possible. When the original employs iambic pentameter, this translation does too. When characters speak in prose, the translation shifts to prose. Rhymes, the occasional alliteration, and metrical irregularities remain. Jokes, inspired or lame, and poetic devices get modern equivalents. Sentence length and syntactic complexity are the same.

No doubt this translation has changes that may disturb purists. For example, I abandon the distinction between *you* (formal/distant/deferential) and *thou* (familiar/condescending/insulting). For Elizabethan audiences, this distinction, although losing force in everyday speech, still revealed information about class and speaker attitude. Today the distinction is obscure, and the use of *thou* achieves the opposite of Shakespeare's intention. For at least three hundred years the *Thou/thee/thy/thine* paradigm has been confined to poetry, religious expression, and solemn, formal oratory. No matter how many reminders are offered, few modern readers will

7

feel tension when a commoner addresses a noble as "thou" and may even misinterpret it as formal, elevated address. I have to signal disrespect in some other way. Remember that this translation wants the drama to come to life for modern audiences, not serve as a primer in the English of Queen Elizabeth I.

To help comprehension, I occasionally add brief pieces of exposition, careful to operate within the metrical constraints imposed by the original. Shakespeare occasionally makes references to Greek mythology and folk legends, many of which are obscure today. So "Bellona" becomes "warrior goddess," or "Graymalkin" becomes "the gray cat." This practice eliminates the need for footnotes, which are unavailable to the theater audience and a distraction to readers. The occasional endnote offers an alternate translation of a disputed passage or explains a decision to deviate from the original. Readers can ignore endnotes without loss of comprehension.

I suggest reading the translation without referring to the original so that you can imagine the play as theater in real time with the rhythm and pacing undisturbed. Don't be surprised if the "colors" seem a bit brighter than you remember them. After four centuries, more than a little "linguistic grime" builds up as our language changes. Keep in mind how surprised we are when Renaissance paintings are restored to their original state and those muted, sepia hues turn into celebrations of color. My translation wants you to see the same colors that the groundlings and the royalty saw when they crowded into theaters 400 years ago.

Kent Richmond
Lakewood, California

Notes on the Meter

Shakespeare's plays mix blank verse (unrhymed iambic pentameter), prose, and songs. They also include couplets or other rhyme schemes to close scenes and heighten dramatic exchanges. This translation preserves these forms, assuming Shakespeare had a dramatic justification for these swings between blank verse, prose, and rhyme.

In translating songs, I mimic the rhythm and find suitable rhymes, but Shakespeare's blank verse is more problematic and requires decisions as to what constitutes a metrical line. His plays, especially the later ones, are full of short and long lines, lines with extra syllables, and other deviations from the expected ten-syllable line. If a line deviates, was Shakespeare sloppy? Is the text corrupt? Has the pronunciation changed? Or was he aiming for some dramatic effect?

Shakespeare did not leave us polished editions of his plays. But several hundred years of tinkering by scholars has provided the polishing and copy editing that Shakespeare failed to do. I take advantage of that scholarship and assume that any remaining anomalies are part of Shakespeare's design and must be respected. If the deviant meter is due to pronunciation change, then I find a metrical equivalent in contemporary English. If not, then the translation deviates in the same way as the original.

Of course no translation can perfectly capture both the sense and sound of poetry. When conflicts arise, I favor sense over strict adherence to the rhythm. Yet I do not allow a line to have a rhythm not found in Shakespeare's verse at the time he wrote the play.

For more information on Shakespeare's verse, see "Appendix 1: How Iambic Pentameter Works."

About the Play

Shakespeare's *Macbeth* is a fast-paced, intensely poetic account of the rise and fall of a murderous Scottish nobleman. The story comes from the 1587 edition of Raphael Holinshed's *Chronicles of England, Scotland, and Ireland*, a popular three-volume history full of facts, legends, and interesting plots. Shakespeare combined several of the *Chronicles'* tales to create the composite character of Macbeth and the fictional Lady Macbeth, Macbeth's accomplice in his reign of terror. Macbeth was an actual historical character who ruled Scotland in the mid 11th century, but given the inaccuracies in Holinshed's fantasy-tinged history and Shakespeare's melding of separate historical events, the play becomes a work of fiction.

It is not certain when the play was written and first performed. There are no records of its performance before 1611, and the earliest known print copy dates to 1623. Given its Scottish location and the parade of Scottish Kings in Act 4, most scholars agree it was written no earlier than 1603, when James Stuart, King of the Scots, ascended the throne to become King James I of England. The generous use of witchcraft also suggests an appeal to the interests of James, who had written a book on the subject in 1597. It is interesting to note that these spooky witchcraft scenes proved so popular that later adaptations expanded them to allow for elaborate stage effects. These additions worked so well that productions today often include the material even though we know Shakespeare did not write it.

For centuries, scholars and fans have debated the circumstances and motivations that accompany Macbeth's descent into evil. One view is that Macbeth was at first a good man, a brave and competent general who suppressed a rebellion in support of a beneficent and popular king. Excited by three manipulative witches who predict he will be king and goaded by his wife, Macbeth succumbs to what he calls "vaulting ambition." He then kills or slanders all those who stand between himself and the throne. At first Macbeth hides from his conscience by imagining himself in a trancelike state as he commits his first murders—the deeds just happen. Later he uses proxies. Lady Macbeth believes suppressing sympathetic feeling is the key. None of these tactics work. We watch as the two villains, besieged by guilt and fear, crack under the pressure of fighting off both their consciences and the many enemies they have created.

The beauty of Shakespeare's poetry is enough to sustain our interest if the play is this straightforward. But there is still the matter of Macbeth's motivation. How could a good man fall so quickly? Macbeth offers no justification for murder except ambition. No one has betrayed him or broken a promise. His ideology seems identical to his peers. He does not have a chip on his shoulder, he lives in a lovely place, and he has a loyal wife. If the witches are correct, and he believes they are, he will become king soon enough. King Duncan is old, and we later learn that Malcolm, his eldest son, is unsure of his moral fitness and is ready to abdicate. If Macbeth thinks it through, he only needs to wait. The witches tell him that Banquo's descendants will succeed him, but Macbeth has no children of his own, so why is Banquo a threat?

Perhaps we should take a closer look at Macbeth's world. Is it one where patience is a winning strategy? The leaders are all warriors. King Duncan seems honest and admirable, yet he has just put down a rebellion led by a Thane in league with a foreign king. Too old to fight himself, Duncan holds onto his reign by awarding favors to those who loyally support him in battle. It is a world where leadership, manliness, and wealth are tied to bravery in battle and the defense of fiefdoms through bloodshed. In such a climate—the words *blood/bloody/bloodier/bleed/bleeding* appear nearly 50 times in the play—Macbeth's actions seem plausible.

Of course, the unstable and volatile political situation of Scotland does not excuse Macbeth's crimes. Seasoned warriors are sickened by his excesses. Macduff, in particular, pays dearly for underestimating the extent of Macbeth's savagery. And even the most peaceful places can be disturbed by a sociopath who goes on a murder spree, so we do not need the presence of a warrior culture to explain the existence of homicide. But it does help explain how someone like Macbeth could rise as high as he did and why Lady Macbeth, physically and socially incapable of causing or ordering violent death herself, sees Macbeth's violence as the only instrument through which a married woman can quickly rise to the top.

Macbeth is a strange play, and modern readers may have trouble coming to terms with its supernatural elements. The skeptical can explain away floating daggers, ghosts, and indelible bloodstains as delusions. Reports of cannibalistic horses could be exaggeration. But the witches are real. They open the play, and both Banquo and Macbeth see them. Did Shakespeare believe that sorcery played a role in Scotland's history? We know that King James blamed witches for calamities (though he was more skeptical later in life), Holinshed's *Chronicle* included them, and audiences of the day were open to such possibilities. As you read, consider whether the witches control events or whether they merely celebrate what is likely. Are their words predictions or instructions?

As in many Shakespeare plays, language itself is an accomplice in the conflict. Both Macbeth and his comical porter complain about equivocation—that is, using one word in two different senses. The porter sees "equivocators" as frauds who belong in hell. Macbeth discovers that the witches change the sense of words to trick him without actually lying. But what about this prophecy? "No one of woman born shall harm Macbeth." Is anyone who threatens Macbeth not "of woman born?" Banquo warns Macbeth early in the play:

> But it's strange—
> That oftentimes to lure us into harm,
> The instruments of darkness tell us truths,
> Lure us with trivial facts, betraying us
> When consequences matter most.

In a play about unconscionable betrayal, do the spirits betray Macbeth with the truth or with a lie?

Characters in the Play

DUNCAN, King of Scotland
MALCOLM, his son
DONALBAIN, his son

Macbeth's Household
  MACBETH, a General in King Duncan's Army
  LADY MACBETH, Macbeth's wife
  GENTLEWOMAN, serving Lady Macbeth
  A **DOCTOR,** serving Lady Macbeth
  A **PORTER**
  three **ASSASSINS,** serving Macbeth
  SEYTON, an officer serving Macbeth

Other Scottish Nobles
  MACDUFF, a Nobleman
  LADY MACDUFF, his wife
  MACDUFF'S SON
  BANQUO, a General in the King's Army
  FLEANCE, his son
  LENNOX, a Nobleman
  ROSS, a Nobleman
  MENTEITH, a Nobleman
  ANGUS, a Nobleman
  CAITHNESS, a Nobleman

Supernatural Beings and Ghosts
  Three **WITCHES**
  HECATE
  GHOST OF BANQUO
  APPARITIONS: a head, a bloody child, a crowned child,
  eight kings

A **CAPTAIN** in Duncan's army
SIWARD, Commander of the English Forces
  YOUNG SIWARD, his son

An English **DOCTOR**
an **OLD MAN**

**ATTENDANTS, MESSENGERS, SERVANTS, A BUTLER,
SOLDIERS, LORDS, ASSASSINS**

SCENE
11th-century Scotland.
Act 4, Scene 3 takes place in England.

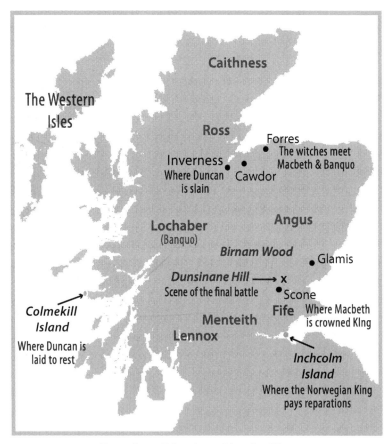

Locations Mentioned in the Play

Macbeth

Act One

Act One

Scene One. An Open Place Outdoors

[Thunder and lightning. Enter three WITCHES]

FIRST WITCH
When shall we three meet again?
In thunder, lightning, or in rain?

SECOND WITCH
When the hurly-burly's done,
When the battle's lost and won.

THIRD WITCH
Before the setting of the sun.   5

FIRST WITCH
Where's the place?

SECOND WITCH
Out on the heath.

THIRD WITCH
It's there we meet Macbeth.

FIRST WITCH
The gray cat calls!

SECOND WITCH
I hear the toad.   10

THIRD WITCH
It's time.

ALL THREE
Fair is foul, and foul is fair.
Hover in the fog and filthy air.

[Exit WITCHES]

Scene Two. A Camp

[A trumpet call is heard. Enter DUNCAN, MALCOLM,
DONALBAIN, LENNOX, with ATTENDANTS, meeting
a bleeding CAPTAIN]

DUNCAN (King of Scotland)
Who is this bloody man? Perhaps he can,
To judge from his condition, give us news
On this revolt.

MALCOLM (Duncan's Son)
           This is the officer
Who, as all good and hardy soldiers do,
Fought off my captors—Hail, brave friend!   5
Share with the king your knowledge of the battle
Up to the time you left.

CAPTAIN (serving in Duncan's army)
           Uncertain....[1]
Like worn-out swimmers who discard their skills
And choke each other. Merciless Macdonald—
Well-suited for revolt and swarming with   10
The multiplying evils spawned by nature—
From Scotland's Western Isles had received
Ax-wielding horseman and light infantry,
And fortune, like a rebel's whore, smiled on
His hateful cause. But he was still too weak,   15
For brave Macbeth—a label much deserved—
Disdaining fortune's smile, with brandished steel,
Now steaming from its bloody enterprise

Like valor's favorite child...carved out a passage
Till he faced the villain...   20
And never shook his hand or bid farewell,
Till he had ripped a seam from chin to navel,
And stuck his head on top our battlements.

DUNCAN
O valiant kinsman! Worthy gentleman!

CAPTAIN
From where the suns begins its northward climb[2]   25
Shipwrecking storms and dreadful thunder come,
And from the spring that seemed to offer hope,
Despair wells up. So heed this, King of Scotland:
The moment justice, armed with valor, made
The light-armed Celts turn on their heels and run,   30
The King of Norway, seeing an advantage,
With polished arms and new supplies of men,
Began a fresh assault.

DUNCAN
And did our generals panic, Macbeth and Banquo?[3]

CAPTAIN
Yes....If sparrows scare hawks or rabbits lions.   35
If I speak truly, I can say they were
Like cannons loaded with a double charge,
First doubling then redoubling strokes upon their foes—
If they desired to bathe in smoldering wounds,
Or make the field as famed as Calvary   40
I cannot tell—
But I am faint. My gashes cry for help.

DUNCAN
These words you speak adorn your wounds so well
Both taste of honor.—Go and get him surgeons.

[Exit CAPTAIN, helped out by attendants]

Who's coming now?

MALCOLM

The worthy Thane of Ross.   45

LENNOX (a Nobleman of Scotland)
What haste shows through his eyes! As one might look
Who's come to say strange things.

[Enter ROSS]

ROSS (A Nobleman of Scotland)

God save the King!

DUNCAN
Where have you come from, worthy thane?

ROSS

From Fife,
Great king, where Norway's banners mock the sky
And fan our people cold.   50
There Norway's King, with terrifying numbers,
Assisted by the most disloyal of traitors,
The Thane of Cawdor, began an ominous onslaught
Until the warrior goddess sent her man
In tested armor and with equal skill   55
To face him, spear to spear and arm to arm,
Curbing his reckless spirit. And, to conclude,
The victory went to us.

DUNCAN

Great happiness!

ROSS
Now Sweno, Norway's king, has asked for terms.
We won't allow the burial of his men   60
Until he's paid to us at Inchcolm Island
Ten thousand silver coins for public use.

DUNCAN
The Thane of Cawdor won't betray again
My deepest trust.—Immediate death for him,
And use his title when you greet Macbeth.   65

ROSS
I'll see it's done.

DUNCAN
What he has lost, noble Macbeth has won.

[Exit]

Scene Three. A Heath

[Thunder. Enter the three WITCHES]

FIRST WITCH
Where have you been, sister?

SECOND WITCH
Killing pigs.

THIRD WITCH
Sister, where were you?

FIRST WITCH
A sailor's wife had chestnuts in her lap,
And munched, and munched, and munched—"They're
    mine," says I.   5
"Away, you witch!" the flab-fed floozy cries.
Aleppo's where her husband's gone, captain of the Tiger,
But in a sieve that's how I'll sail,
And be a rat without a tail,
And get him, get him, get him.   10

SECOND WITCH
I'll make you a breeze.

FIRST WITCH
If you please.

THIRD WITCH
And I one from the west.

FIRST WITCH
While I myself control the rest,
And from the ports themselves they'll blow   15
All the compass points they know
On the seaman's charts.
He shall live a man who's cursed,
His hanging tongue will truly thirst
For I will drain him dry as hay,   20
No sleep for him night or day.
Weary sixty nights times nine,
He will dwindle, waste, and pine.
No, his vessel won't be lost,
But it will be tempest-tossed.   25
Look what I have.

SECOND WITCH
Show me, show me.

FIRST WITCH
Here's a shipwrecked pilot's thumb,
Floating homeward in the scum.

[A drum is heard]

THIRD WITCH
A drum, a drum!   30
Macbeth has come.

ALL
[dancing in a circle] We weird sisters, hand in hand,
Race across the sea and land,
This is how we get about.
Three times yours, and three times mine,   35
And three again, to make it nine.
Peace, the spell's all set.

[Enter MACBETH and BANQUO]

MACBETH (a General in King Duncan's army)
A day this fair and foul I have not seen.

BANQUO (a General in King Duncan's army)
How far is Forres from here?—What are these,
Too withered and too wild in their attire   40
To be inhabiting this earth and yet
They're here?—[to the WITCHES] Are you alive? Or things
    with which
I can converse? You seem to understand me,
For all at once you placed a shriveled finger
Upon your skinny lips. You must be women,   45
And yet your beards do not let me conclude
That you are so.

MACBETH
                        Speak, if you can. What are you?

FIRST WITCH
All hail, Macbeth! Hail to thee, Thane of Glamis!

SECOND WITCH
All hail, Macbeth! Hail to thee, Thane of Cawdor!

THIRD WITCH
All hail, Macbeth! Who is the king to be!   50

BANQUO
Good sir, why did you flinch and seem to fear
These things that sound so good?—[to the WITCHES] I
    need the truth—
Are you imaginary, or just what
You seem to be? You greet my noble partner
By current rank and with such great predictions   55
Of noble titles gained and royal hopes
That he's entranced.—To me you do not speak.
If you can look into the seeds of time,
And say which grain will grow and which will not,
Then speak to one who does not ask for favors   60
And does not fear your hate.

FIRST WITCH
Hail!

SECOND WITCH
Hail!

THIRD WITCH
Hail!

FIRST WITCH
Lesser than Macbeth, and greater. 65

SECOND WITCH
Not so well-off, yet better off.

THIRD WITCH
You will spawn kings, yet not be one.
So all hail, Macbeth and Banquo!

FIRST WITCH
Banquo and Macbeth, all hail!

MACBETH
Your story is not clear yet. Tell me more. 70
My father's death makes me the Thane of Glamis—
But Cawdor? The Thane of Cawdor is alive,
A prosperous gentleman, and to be king
Lies far outside the limits of belief,
More so than even Cawdor.[4] Give a source 75
For your strange information, or state why
You blocked our path across this barren heath
With such prophetic greetings?—Speak, I say.

[the WITCHES vanish]

BANQUO
The earth has bubbles, just as water does,
And that's what these must be. Where did they go? 80

MACBETH
Into the air, and what seemed solid vanished
Like breath into the wind.—I wish they'd stayed!

BANQUO
Were these things we're discussing really here?
Or did some root we ate make us insane
And take our reason prisoner?   85

MACBETH
Your children will be kings.

BANQUO
                              You will be king.

MACBETH
And how'd it go? The Thane of Cawdor too?

BANQUO
That is the tune and words I heard. Who's this?

[Enter ROSS and ANGUS]

ROSS
The king, Macbeth, has happily received
The news of your success, and when he sees   90
The risks you took in fighting the rebellion,
His admiration and astonishment
Compete for words.[5] And silenced by all that,
Reviewing other news from that same day,
He knows you faced the brave Norwegian line,   95
Not fearing for yourself what they'd become—
Strange, deathly likenesses. As thick as hail[6]
Came message after message, pouring praise
Around him, telling how your great defense
Preserved his kingdom.

ANGUS (a Nobleman of Scotland)
                              And so we are here   100
To give to you our royal master's thanks,
Though not to pay you now, but summon you
To see him.

ROSS
And as a promise of much greater honors,

He's ordered me to call you Thane of Cawdor,   105
And hail you with that title, worthy thane,
For it is yours.

BANQUO
                    Can devils speak the truth?

MACBETH
The Thane of Cawdor lives. Why dress me up
In borrowed robes?

ANGUS
                    The former Thane still lives,
But now that life, which he deserves to lose,   110
Received a heavy sentence. Whether he
Conspired with Norway, backed the rebel up
With hidden reinforcements, or did both
To seek to wreck his country, I don't know.
But treason's verdict—death—confessed and proved,   115
Has toppled him.

MACBETH
                    [Aside] Glamis, and Thane of Cawdor.
The greatest is to come. [to ROSS and ANGUS]—Thanks
    for your pains.—
[Privately to BANQUO] Now don't you hope your children
    will be kings,
When those who said they'd make me Thane of Cawdor
Promised no less to them.

BANQUO
                    Full trust in that   120
May well ignite your hopes of being king,
Besides the Thane of Cawdor. But it's strange—
That oftentimes to lure us into harm,
The instruments of darkness tell us truths,
Lure us with trivial facts, betraying us   125
When consequences matter most.—
Cousins, a word with you please. [BANQUO, ROSS, and
    ANGUS step aside]

MACBETH
          [Aside] Two truths are told,
Both lucky prologues as the drama builds
On this imperial theme. [to the others]—I thank you,
   gentlemen.—
[Aside] This supernatural effort to entice   130
Cannot be evil, can't be good. If evil,
Why has it brought this promise of reward,
Commencing with a truth? I am Thane of Cawdor.
If good, why do I yield to this temptation
Whose hideous image stands my hair on end,   135
And makes my once-firm heart knock on my ribs
In this unnatural way? The fears at hand
Are less than any horror we imagine.
My thoughts, where murder's still no more than fantasy,
Shake loose my fragile hold so much[7]   140
That functioning is swamped by speculation.
And nothing is—except what isn't yet.

BANQUO
Our partner seems entranced.

MACBETH
[Aside] If chance says I'll be king, then chance can crown
   me
Without my efforts.

BANQUO
          He's trying on new honors,   145
Which like new clothes, won't stretch to our physique
Unless we put them on.

MACBETH
          [Aside] Then come what may,
For time keeps running through the roughest day.

BANQUO
Worthy Macbeth, we'll leave when you are ready.

MACBETH

Indulge me just a bit. Forgotten things   150
Are stirring this dull brain. Kind gentlemen,
The pains you took are now recorded where
I'll read them everyday—Now to the king.—
[To BANQUO] Reflect on what's occurred. When there's
    been time
To weigh it in the interim, let our hearts   155
Speak freely to each other.

BANQUO
                Very gladly.

MACBETH
Till then, enough.—Come, friends.

               [Exit]

Scene Four. A Room in Forres Castle

    [Trumpets sound. Enter DUNCAN, MALCOLM,
      DONALBAIN, LENNOX, and ATTENDANTS]

DUNCAN

Was Cawdor's execution carried out?
Have those assigned to do it come back yet?

MALCOLM

My king, not yet. But I have spoken with
A man who saw him die, who can report
That Cawdor openly confessed his treason,   5
Asked for a pardon from you, and expressed
A deep repentance. Nothing in his life
Suits him as well as leaving it. He died
A man who knew his dying lines so well,
He threw away the dearest thing he owned   10
Like some mere trifle.

DUNCAN
                              There's no skill that helps
Us find the mind's intention in a face.
He was a gentleman on whom I built
An absolute trust.—

[Enter MACBETH, BANQUO, ROSS, and ANGUS]

                              O worthiest cousin!
The sin of my ingratitude to you   15
Still weighs me down. You've moved ahead so fast,
The swiftest-flying recompense takes long
To overtake you. If you deserved much less,
My payment and my thanks to you could be
The right proportion. All that's left to say   20
Is you are due much more than I can pay.

MACBETH
The service and the loyalty I owe,
Once paid, rewards itself. Your role is to
Receive our loyalty, a duty owed
To throne and state like those a child or servant   25
Must owe if they by owing everything
Preserve your love and honor.

DUNCAN
                              Welcome here.
Your nurturing has begun, and I will work
To help you reach full growth.—My, noble Banquo,
Who has achieved no less and must be known   30
No less for doing so, let me embrace you
And hold you near my heart.

BANQUO
                              If I grow there,
The harvest goes to you.

DUNCAN
                              This lavish joy,
So unrestrained, now seeks to hide itself

In tears of sorrow. [pauses]—Sons, kinsmen, thanes,   35
And others nearest to the throne, hear this:
I name as my successor to this realm
My eldest, Malcolm, who shall now be known
As Prince of Cumberland; which does not mean
That honors will be worn by him alone,   40
But symbols of nobility, like stars,
Shall shine on the deserving. To Inverness,
Where our debt to you grows.

MACBETH
Rest makes us weary if we cannot serve you.
I'll go ahead alone so that my wife   45
Can hear the joyful news of your approach.
I humbly take my leave.

DUNCAN
                    My worthy Cawdor!

MACBETH
[Aside, while DUNCAN and BANQUO converse] The Prince
    of Cumberland!—That is one step
That I must skip or I will surely fall,
For it lies in my way. Stars, hide your fires!   50
No light must see my black and deep desires:
The eye ignores the hand, and leaves it be
To do the very thing it fears to see.

                    [Exit]

DUNCAN
True, worthy Banquo!—There's no doubt he's valiant,
And on your praise for him I am well-fed.   55
To me, it is a banquet.—Let's follow him,
Whose kindness rushed him off to welcome us,
A kinsman without peers.

                [Trumpets sound. Exit]

Scene Five. Inverness. In Macbeth's Castle

[Enter LADY MACBETH, reading a letter]

LADY MACBETH (Macbeth's Wife)
[Reads] *"They met me on the day of our victory, and I*
learned from their very clear account that they have
more in them than what is known to mortals. I was
burning with desire to question them further, but they
turned themselves into air and vanished. While I stood   5
there rapt in the wonder of it, messengers from the king
came and said 'All Hail Thane of Cawdor,' the same
title the weird sisters used before they looked farther
ahead with their 'Hail, king to be!' I thought it would
be good to inform you of this, my dearest partner in   10
greatness, so you will not miss the joy you are due by
being ignorant of the greatness promised to you. Con-
sider this carefully, and farewell."

Glamis you are, and Cawdor, and will be
What's promised, yet your nature worries me.   15
It's too full of the milk of human kindness
To snatch the quickest means. Your wish for fame
Is not without ambition, but you lack
The wickedness required. You wish to gain
Your highest wish through righteousness, not guile,   20
And yet you'd cheat to win. You need, great Glamis,
A voice that cries, "Then do it," if you seek it,
And do that thing you fear to do more than
You wish it were not done. Go there at once
So I may pour my spirit in your ear   25
And chastise with the valor of my tongue
Whatever keeps you from the golden crown,
Which fate and supernatural help seem sure
To place upon your head.

[Enter a MESSENGER]

Yes, any news?

MESSENGER
The king arrives tonight.

LADY MACBETH
                              You must be joking.   30
Your master's with him, isn't he? If so,
He'd send us word so that we could prepare.

MESSENGER
You will be pleased to know—our thane is coming.
One of my comrades raced ahead of him,
And gasping to get air had breath enough   35
To get this message out.

LADY MACBETH
                              Go tend to him.
He brings great news.

                    [Exit MESSENGER]

                              The raven will grow hoarse
From cawing Duncan's fatal movement here
Beneath my battlements. Come, you spirits
Who act on murderous thoughts, unsex me here   40
And fill me up from crown to toe, chock-full
Of the most dreadful cruelty. Freeze my blood,
Stop up all passageways to tenderness
So no compassion from within me leaks
To shake my fierce resolve and keep it from   45
Its full effect! Come to this woman's breasts,
And trade my milk for bile, you murdering minions,
Wherever you invisible attendants
Are serving nature's mayhem! Come, deep night,
And wrap yourself in hell's most dismal pall   50
So my quick knife can't see the wound it makes
And heaven can't peer through the dark's thick sheet
To cry, "Halt, halt!"

                    [Enter MACBETH]

Great Glamis! Worthy Cawdor!
Greater than both when we can hear "All Hail!"
Your letter has transported me beyond   55
My present ignorance, and I now feel
The future is at hand.

MACBETH
                    My dearest love,
Duncan arrives tonight.

LADY MACBETH
                    When does he leave?

MACBETH
Tomorrow's his intention.

LADY MACBETH
                    Never shall
He see tomorrow's sun!   60
Your face, my thane, is like a book where men
Can read the news. Your presence will deceive
Those present if there's welcome in your eyes,
Your hand, your mouth. Look like an innocent flower,
But be the snake beneath it. Let's prepare   65
For who is coming here, but you must leave
The planning for tonight's great task to me,
Which will for every future day and hour,
Grant solely to us full and sovereign power.

MACBETH
Let's think this over.

LADY MACBETH
                    Just look full of cheer.   70
A changed expression usually signals fear.
Leave all the rest to me.

[Exit]

Scene Six. Outside Macbeth's Castle

[Hautboys (loud double-reed musical instruments) are
heard. SERVANTS of Macbeth are waiting]

[Enter DUNCAN, MALCOLM, DONALBAIN,
BANQUO, LENNOX, MACDUFF, ROSS, ANGUS,
and ATTENDANTS]

DUNCAN
This castle's in a pleasant site. The air—
So fresh and sweet—is quite agreeable
And soothing to our senses.

BANQUO
              [sees a bird] This guest of summer,
The tower-loving swallow, proves indeed
From where he builds his nest, that heaven's breath   5
Invites us here. No buttresses or frescos,
No ledge or sheltered corner, yet he's made
A hanging bed and cradle for his young.
Wherever these birds breed, I've noticed that
The air's delightful.   10

[Enter LADY MACBETH]

DUNCAN
Look, here's our honored hostess!—
This love I get may sometimes seem a bother,
Yet I still thank this love. In saying this,
You'll learn that burdens such as these are gifts
And thank me for these pains.

LADY MACBETH
              These preparations,   15
With every stitch done twice and then redoubled,
Are poor and threadbare efforts that can't match
The deep, extensive honors of our king
That now adorn our house. For honors old

And recent ones just added to the pile,   20
Our prayers continue.

DUNCAN
              Where's the Thane of Cawdor?
I followed at his heels and hoped I could
Prepare his welcome here; but he rides well,
And his great love, sharp as his spur, helped him
Reach home before us. Fair and noble hostess,   25
I am your guest tonight.

LADY MACBETH
              Your servants keep
A full account of all they have—themselves,
Their staff, their property—so that our king
May use them at his pleasure.

DUNCAN
              Give me your hand;
Escort me to my host. We love him highly   30
And will continue our appreciation.
With your permission, hostess.

[Exit]

Scene Seven. In Macbeth's Castle

[Hautboys are heard. Torches visible]
[The head BUTLER and several SERVANTS enter with
dishes and food to be served, cross the room, and exit.
Then enter MACBETH]

MACBETH
If it is done when done, then it is best
If it's done quickly. If dispatching him[8]
Could haul in every consequence, and seize,
Once he has ceased, success, and if this blow
Could be the be-all and the end-all—here,   5

Right here, upon this bank, this shoal of time— 9
Then why not risk our souls? But in this case
We might be punished here, in that this is
A bloody lesson, which once taught, returns
To plague its author. Balanced retribution   10
Would raise the liquids in our poisoned chalice
To our own lips. He's doubly in my trust:
The fact that he's my kinsman and my king
Strikes hard against this deed. Then, as his host,
I should prevent this death and bar the door,   15
Not hold the knife myself. Besides, King Duncan
Has been so humble in his use of power,
So blameless in high office that his virtues
Like angels, trumpet-tongued, will plead against
The deep damnation of removing him.   20
And pity, like a naked new-born babe,
Riding this blast, or cherubs from above
On unseen carriers of the air will blow
This horrid deed into so many eyes
That tears will drown the wind. I have no spur   25
To prod the flanks of my intent but one—
Vaulting ambition, which leaps past itself
To fall down on the other....

[Enter LADY MACBETH]

Here you are? Any news?

LADY MACBETH
He's dining still. Why have you left the chamber?   30

MACBETH
He asked for me?

LADY MACBETH
                Of course, you know he has.

MACBETH
We will proceed no further in this business.
He's honoring me right now, and I have won

Golden acclaim from people of all ranks,
Which should be worn while it still has its gloss,   35
Not cast aside so soon.

LADY MACBETH
                              Was your hope drunk
When you got dressed in it? Did it pass out
And wake just now to look so green and pale
At what it did so freely? From now on,
That's how I'll see your love. Are you afraid   40
To be the same in action and in valor
As you are in your dreams? Can you wish for
What you regard as life's most cherished prize,
Yet live a coward in your own regard,
Like the poor cat that "wished" to eat the fish,   45
But "dared not" get its feet wet.

MACBETH
                              Please, enough.
I dare to do what makes me be a man.
Who dares do more is not.

LADY MACBETH
                              What beast was it
That let me in on this great enterprise?
You dared to do that, and you were a man.   50
And if that made you more a man, you will
Be even more. When neither time nor place
Seemed advantageous, you set out to fix that.
Now that conditions line themselves up well,
You are upset. I've shared my milk and know   55
How sweet it is to love a nursing babe.
And yet, while it is smiling up at me,
I'd pluck my nipple from its boneless gums
And dash its brains out if, as you have done,
I'd said I'd do it.

MACBETH
                    But if we fail?

LADY MACBETH
                We fail? 60
Just wind your courage till you hear it click,[10]
And we won't fail. When Duncan's sound asleep—
A state encouraged all the sooner by
Today's hard journey—his two chamber guards
I'll overcome with so much wine and cheer 65
That memory, the guardian of the brain,
Will turn to fumes, with reason's reservoir
A duct to vent it. When in sluggish sleep
Their drink-drenched beings lie as if they're dead,
Is there one thing that you and I can't do 70
To an unguarded Duncan? Why not lay
Upon his soggy officers the guilt
Of our great kill?

MACBETH
              Bring forth men-children only,
For your undaunted mettle will produce
Nothing but males. Will there be any doubt, 75
Once we have stained this sleepy duo with blood
In his own room and used their knives to do it,
That they're the cause?

LADY MACBETH
                And who would dare to doubt it,
If we can make our grief and outcry roar
Upon his death?

MACBETH
              I'm set on it and twist 80
Each fiber in me toward this terrible deed.
Away, delude the world, put on a show.
False faces have to hide what false hearts know.

              [Exit]

Macbeth

Act Two

Act Two

Scene One. A Courtyard in Macbeth's Castle

[Enter BANQUO, preceded by FLEANCE,
carrying a torch]

BANQUO
How long till morning, boy?

FLEANCE (Banquo's Son)
The moon is down. I have not heard the clock.

BANQUO
And she goes down at twelve.

FLEANCE
I think, it's later, sir.

BANQUO
Here, take my sword. [Hands FLEANCE his sword] The
   night is cutting costs.   5
Its candles are all out. And hold this too. [hands FLEANCE
   a small case]
Sleep's heavy summons lies like lead upon me,
Yet I can't rest. Merciful powers above,
Protect me from the horrid thoughts our minds
Give way to when we doze!—Give me my sword.   10

[Enter MACBETH, and a SERVANT with a torch]

Who's there?

MACBETH
A friend.

BANQUO
What, sir, not yet asleep? The king's in bed.
He's been extremely pleased and has bestowed
Some generous gifts on all your household staff.   15
This diamond's yours in recognition of
Your wife's kind hospitality, encased
In boundless gratitude. [hands MACBETH the case that
    FLEANCE is holding]

MACBETH
                        Caught unprepared,
Our wish to entertain without restraint
Was bound by certain limits.

BANQUO
                        All's well.   20
I dreamt last night about those three weird sisters.
In your case, they seemed right.

MACBETH
                        They don't concern me.
Yet, when we find an hour or so to speak,
Let's spend it sharing thoughts about these matters,
If you will spare the time.

BANQUO
                        At your kind pleasure.   25

MACBETH
If you embrace my interests—when it's time,
There will be honors for you.

BANQUO
                        As long as I
Lose none in seeking more but always keep
My conscious free and my allegiance clear,
Then I will follow.

MACBETH

In the meantime rest! 30

BANQUO
Thanks, sir. You do that too!

[Exit BANQUO and FLEANCE]

MACBETH
Go tell your mistress, when my drink is ready,
To ring the bell. Then you may go to bed.

[Exit SERVANT]

Is this a dagger that I see before me,
The handle toward my hand? Here, let me clutch you.   35
I do not have you, yet I see you still.
Are you not, fatal vision, evident
To touch as well as sight? Or are you but
A dagger in my mind, a false illusion,
Emerging from an overheated brain?   40
And yet this form looks just as tangible
As this one I now draw. [draws his dagger]
You guide me down the path that I was going
And are the instrument I was to use.
My eyes are either fools or worth more than   45
My other senses. I can see you still,
And on the blade and hilt are clots of blood,
Which were not there before.—There's no such thing.
It is this bloody business which has done
This to my eyes. Across the world's dark half,   50
Nature seems dead, encased in sleep, deceived
By wicked dreams. The sorcerer's goddess Hecate
Receives the witches' offering, and gaunt Murder,
Alerted by his sentinel, the wolf,
Its howl his timepiece, at a stealthy pace,   55
Moves ghostlike, with a rapist's wary stride,
In on his prey. O, firm and stable earth,
Don't hear my steps, or how they walk, for fear
These stones of yours will leak my whereabouts

And break the ghastly silence of this hour,   60
Which suits this deed. While I make threats, he lives.
Cold wind to cool hot deeds is all talk gives.

[A bell chimes]

I'll go, and then it's done. That chime's my signal.
Don't hear it, Duncan, for it is the bell
That summons you to heaven or to hell.   65

[Exit]

Scene Two. Inside Macbeth's Castle

[Enter LADY MACBETH]

LADY MACBETH
That which has made them drunk has made me bold.
What's doused their flame has brought me fire.—What?—
    Nothing!
An owl just screeched, the bell for the condemned,
The harshest of good nights. He's doing it.
The doors are open, and the stuffed attendants   5
Scoff at their job with snores. I've drugged their
    nightcaps,
So nature's forces battle here to see
If they will live or die.

[MACBETH is heard from beyond a door]

MACBETH
                Who's there?—What's that?

LADY MACBETH
Oh, no! I am afraid they've woken up
And it's not done. Attempt without the deed   10
Will wreck us.—Listen!—I laid out their daggers.

He couldn't miss them.—Had he not resembled
My father as he slept, I would have done it.
My husband?

[Enter MACBETH, holding bloody daggers]

MACBETH
I've done the deed. Did you hear any noise?   15

LADY MACBETH
I heard the owl screech and the crickets cry.
You did not speak?

MACBETH
    When?

LADY MACBETH
      Now.

MACBETH
        As I descended?

LADY MACBETH
Yes.

MACBETH
Wait!—The next room, who's in it?

LADY MACBETH
        Donalbain.

MACBETH
[Looking at his hands] This is a sorry sight.   20

LADY MACBETH
A foolish thought, to say a sorry sight.

MACBETH
First one laughed in his sleep, and one cried, "Murder!"
Enough to wake each other. I froze and listened,

But then they said their prayers and settled down
And fell asleep.

LADY MACBETH
$\qquad\qquad$ The two share the same room. $\qquad$ 25

MACBETH
One cried, "God bless us!" The other said, "Amen."
As if they'd seen me with these hangman's hands.
Hearing their fear, I could not say "Amen,"
When they had said, "God bless us."

LADY MACBETH
Don't think too deeply. $\qquad$ 30

MACBETH
But why could I not say the word "Amen?"
I need his blessing most, and yet "Amen"
Stuck in my throat.

LADY MACBETH
$\qquad\qquad$ We must not think about
These deeds this way, or it will drive us mad.

MACBETH
It seemed I heard a voice cry, "Sleep no more! $\qquad$ 35
Macbeth has murdered sleep,"—yes, innocent sleep,
Sleep that rewinds unraveled threads of care,
The death of each day's life, hard work's warm bath,
Salve for hurt minds, and nature's biggest course,
Chief nourishment in life's feast.

LADY MACBETH
$\qquad\qquad$ What do you mean? $\qquad$ 40

MACBETH
Still it cried, "Sleep no more!" to all the house.
"Glamis has murdered sleep, and therefore Cawdor
Shall sleep no more. Macbeth shall sleep no more!"

LADY MACBETH
And who cried out all this? Why, worthy thane,
You will no doubt untwist your noble strength   45
If you're this addle-brained.—Go get some water,
And wash this filthy evidence off your hands.
And why'd you bring these daggers from the room?
They must stay there. Go take them back and smear
Blood on the sleeping men.

MACBETH
                              I can't go back.   50
I am afraid to think what I have done.
I don't dare look.

LADY MACBETH
                    A weakening resolve!
Give me the daggers. The sleeping and the dead
Are merely paintings. Only childish eyes
Will fear the devil's picture. If there's blood,   55
I'll bronze the faces of his servants with it—
It must appear they're guilty.

                    [She exits. Knocking is heard]

MACBETH
                    What's that knocking?
What's wrong with me, when every noise sends panic?
What hands are these? Ha, they've plucked out my eyes!
Could all of Neptune's ocean wash this blood   60
Clean from my hand? No, this, my hand, would cause
A multitude of seas to fleshify,
Turning their green a single shade of red.

                    [Re-enter LADY MACBETH]

LADY MACBETH
My hands are now your color, but I'd be
Ashamed to have a heart this white.

                    [Knocking is heard]

There's knocking   65
At the south entrance. Let's go to our room.
A little water clears us of this deed.
How easy it all is! Your steadiness
Has now deserted you.

[Knocking is heard]

Hear that? More knocking.
Put on your robe, so if we're called upon   70
We'll look as if we've slept. Don't lose yourself
In morbid thoughts.

MACBETH
I cannot face this deed and face myself.[1]

[Knocking is heard]

Wake Duncan with your knocking! I wish you could!

[Exit]

Scene Three. Inside Macbeth's Castle

[Enter a PORTER. Knocking is heard]

PORTER
Wouldn't you know, knocking! A doorman at the gates of
hell would keep plenty busy turning the key.

[Knocking]

Knock, knock, knock. Who's there, in the name of Beelze-
bub? A farmer who hoarded his crops then hung himself
when prices dropped? You've come to the right place. We   5
have plenty of rags to wipe your brow, and here you'll need
them.

[Knocking]

Knock, knock! Who's there, in the name of...of...that other
devil? Ah, here's an equivocator, one who could argue both
sides of his case, commit all sorts of treachery in the name   10
of God, yet could not double talk his way into heaven. Come
on in, equivocator.

[Knocking]

Knock, knock, knock! Who's there? Ah, an English tailor
sent here for skimping on material for the seat of someone's
pants. Come in, tailor. Your iron will keep burning here.   15

[Knocking]

Knock, knock. Never quiet here! What could this be?—
This place is too cold for hell. I'll be the devil's doorman no
further. I'm sure I've let one of every profession walk along
the primrose path to the everlasting bonfire. [Knocking]
Coming, coming! And tip the porter, please.   20

[Opens the gate]
[Enter MACDUFF and LENNOX]

MACDUFF (a Nobleman of Scotland)
Was it because you went to bed so late
That now I catch you lying?

PORTER
The fact is, sir, we were carousing till the cock crowed, and
drink, sir, is a great provoker of three things.

MACDUFF
What three things does drink so expertly provoke?   25

PORTER
Indeed, sir, a painted nose, sleep, and urine. Lechery, sir, it
provokes and unprovokes. It provokes the desire but takes
away the performance. Therefore, heavy drink may be
said to equivocate on the issue of lechery. It builds him up,
and bats him down; says "Sic 'em," and then "down, boy;"   30
it heartens him, and discourages him; makes him stand
straight, and not stand straight; in conclusion, tricks him
into sleeping and leaves him lying.

MACDUFF
I guess drink left you lying flat last night.

PORTER
That it did, sir, by twisting the words in my throat; but I   35
sent his lies back for a refund, and, I think, being too strong
for him, though he got me by the legs for the take-down, I
reversed his move and heaved him.

MACDUFF
Is your master up?—
Our knocking must have woke him. Here he comes.   40

[Enter MACBETH]
[Exit PORTER]]

LENNOX
Good morning, noble sir.

MACBETH

Good morning, sirs.

MACDUFF
Is the king up yet, worthy thane?

MACBETH

Not yet.

MACDUFF
He has commanded me to come by early.
I nearly missed the time.

MACBETH

I'll take you to him.

MACDUFF
I know this is a pleasant nuisance for you,   45
And yet one just the same.

MACBETH
The labors we delight in heal our pains.
Here is the door.

MACDUFF
> I'm sure he will not mind.
Since he assigned this task to me.

> [Exit MACDUFF]

LENNOX
Does the king leave today?   50

MACBETH
He does...he planned to.

LENNOX
The night has been unruly. Where we slept,
Our chimneys were blown down and, some have said,
Laments were in the air, strange screams of death,
And prophesies, in terrifying accents,   55
Of dreadful turmoil and chaotic acts,
Soon hatching in this woeful time. An owl
Shrieked all night long unseen. Some say the earth
Was feverish and shook.

MACBETH
> The night was rough.

LENNOX
My youthful memory can't recall events   60
That can compare.

> [Re-enter MACDUFF]

MACDUFF
> O horror, horror, horror!
No tongue or heart could comprehend or name this!

MACBETH and LENNOX
What's wrong?

MACDUFF
Destruction's masterpiece is now complete!

The most ungodly murder broke inside   65
The Lord's anointed temple, robbing all
The building's life.

MACBETH
     What's this you say? Its life?

LENNOX
You mean his majesty?

MACDUFF
Go in the room, and turn your eyes to stone
With a new Gorgon. Do not ask me more.   70
Look for yourselves.

    [Exit MACBETH and LENNOX]

     Wake up, wake up, wake up!—
Ring the alarm.—There's murder and there's treason!
Banquo and Donalbain! Malcolm! Wake up!
Shake off this down-filled sleep, death's imitation,
And look on death itself! Up, up, and see   75
What doomsday looks like! Malcolm! Banquo!
Rise up as if from death and walk like ghosts
To realize this horror.

    [Alarm bell rings]
    [Enter LADY MACBETH]

LADY MACBETH
     What is all this?
Why such a frightening trumpet to convene
The sleepers of the house? Speak, speak!

MACDUFF
      O gentle lady,   80
It's best that you don't hear what I could say.
Repeating this into a woman's ear
Would murder once its said.

[Re-enter BANQUO]

          O Banquo, Banquo!
Our royal master's murdered!

LADY MACBETH
            Mercy on us!
What, in our house?

BANQUO
          Too cruel anywhere.—   85
Dear Duff, oh please, acknowledge your mistake,
And say it is not so.

[Re-enter MACBETH and LENNOX, with ROSS]

MACBETH
If just one hour before this I had died,
My life would have been blessed. For, from this instant
There's no importance in this mortal life.   90
It's all mere trifles. Fame and grace are dead.
The wine of life's tapped out, and nothing but
The dregs are left to boast of.

[Enter MALCOLM and DONALBAIN]

DONALBAIN
What is amiss?

MACBETH
          You are, and do not know it.
The spring, the head, the fountain of your blood   95
Has stopped; the very source of it has stopped.

MACDUFF
Your royal father's murdered.

MALCOLM
            Oh! By whom?

LENNOX
It seems those in his chamber must have done it.
Their hands and faces wear a badge of blood,
As do their daggers, which, unwiped, we found   100
Upon their pillows.
They stared and looked astonished. No man's life
Should have been in their trust.

MACBETH
And yet I now regret the rage in me
That made me kill them.

MACDUFF
                                        Why did you do that?   105

MACBETH
Who can be wise, and staggered, calmed, and frenzied,
Loyal, and neutral, all at once? No man.
The swiftness of my violent love outruns
The slower pace of reason. There lay Duncan,
His silver skin streaked with his golden blood   110
His gashes like a breech in nature's wall,
Where devastation enters and lays waste.
The murderers, soaked in colors of their trade,
Their daggers sheathed indecently in gore.
Who with a heart of love and courage in it   115
Could not make his love known?

LADY MACBETH
                                        Help me here, huhh!

                    [LADY MACBETH faints]

MACDUFF
Assist the lady.

MALCOLM
                    [Aside to DONALBAIN] Why do we hold our
        tongues
When this event relates to us the most?

DONALBAIN (Duncan's Son)
[Aside to MALCOLM] What can we say when our fate
  too
Hides in some nail hole to lunge and seize us?   120
Let us depart. Our tears need time to brew.

MALCOLM
[Aside to DONALBAIN] And our deep sorrow has not been
  put in motion.

BANQUO
Assist the lady—

       [LADY MACBETH is helped out]

And once we've hid from view the weaknesses
Our half-dressed state's exposed, let us then meet,   125
And look into this bloody piece of work
To better grasp it. Fears and doubts now shake us.
I place myself in God's great hands, and there,
I'll fight against the undisclosed intent
Of this malicious traitor.

MACDUFF
            And I.

ALL
                And all.   130

MACBETH
Let's quickly dress ourselves in proper wear,
And meet together in the hall.

ALL
              Agreed.

    [Exit all but MALCOLM and DONALBAIN]

MALCOLM
What will you do? Let's not join in with them.
To show an unfelt sorrow is behavior
A fraud can easily fake. I'll go to England.   135

DONALBAIN
And me, to Ireland. Taking separate paths
Will keep us safer. There are daggers in
Men's smiles here. Next in line in blood is next
In line to bleed.

MALCOLM
     This murderous arrow's shot
But hasn't landed. And the safest way   140
Is to stay out of range. So let's mount up,
Omit the usual courtesies of leaving,
And just slip out. It's not considered theft
To steal away when there's no mercy left.

       [Exit]

Scene Four. Outside Macbeth's Castle

    [Enter ROSS and an OLD MAN]

OLD MAN
My memory goes back threescore years and ten,
And in that span of time I've surely seen
Grim hours and strange things, but this bleak night
Makes all I've known seem trifling.

ROSS
       Ah, good old man,
Disturbed by man's performance, heaven's dome   5
Threatens to smash this bloody stage. The clock

Says day, yet dark night chokes the wandering light.
Is it night's triumph or the morning's shame
That causes dark to shroud the face of earth
When living light should kiss it?

OLD MAN

It's unnatural,   10
Just like this deed itself. I saw last Tuesday,
A falcon, spiraling to its proudest height,
Attacked and killed by some mouse-catching owl.

ROSS

And Duncan's horses—a thing quite strange yet true—
Though swift and gorgeous, darlings of their breed,   15
Turned wild, broke from their stalls, and kicked and
    bucked,
Rejecting all commands, as if they were
At war with man.

OLD MAN

I heard they ate each other.

ROSS

They did. To the amazement of my eyes,
Which saw it happen.

[Enter MACDUFF]

Ah, here comes good Macduff.   20

How goes the world now, sir?

MACDUFF

Why, can't you see?

ROSS

Have we learned yet who did this bloody deed?

MACDUFF

Those two Macbeth has slain.

ROSS
                    It makes no sense.
What could they gain from it?

MACDUFF
                    The two were bribed.
Malcolm and Donalbain, the king's two sons,   25
Have slipped away and fled, thus placing most
Suspicion onto them.

ROSS
                    It's still not natural.
Pointless ambition—it will gobble up
What life depends on. It's most likely now,
That sovereignty will fall upon Macbeth.   30

MACDUFF
He's just been chosen and has gone to Scone
Where he'll be crowned.

ROSS
                    And where is Duncan's body?

MACDUFF
Carried to Colmekill Island,
The sacred crypt of all his predecessors,
And guardian of their bones.

ROSS
                    And will you go   35
To Scone?

MACDUFF
          No, home to Fife.

ROSS
                    Well, off to Scone.

MACDUFF
Well, maybe things will go well there. Adieu.
I fear our old robes itch less than the new!

ROSS
Farewell, old man.

OLD MAN
God's blessing go with you, as well as those   40
Who will make good from bad and friends from foes!

[Exit]

Macbeth

Act Three

Act Three

Scene One. A Room in Macbeth's Castle at Forres

[Enter BANQUO]

BANQUO
You have it now—King, Cawdor, Glamis, all,
As those weird women promised, and I fear
You played unfair to get it. Yet they said
That this will not be passed on to your heirs,
But I, myself, will be the source and father   5
Of many kings. If more truth comes from them—
And like Macbeth, their words shine bright on me—
To judge by what's become reality,
Why can't their prophecies serve me as well
And raise my hopes? But hush. No more of this.   10

[Trumpets sound. Enter MACBETH as King, LADY
MACBETH as Queen; LENNOX, ROSS, LORDS,
LADIES, and ATTENDANTS]

MACBETH
Here's our main guest.

LADY MACBETH
                    If he had been forgotten,
It would have left a gap in our great feast,
Entirely unbecoming.

MACBETH
Tonight we'll serve a formal banquet, sir,
And I request your presence.

BANQUO
> Let your highness,   15
Command it of a man whose loyalty
Is tied to you forever with a cord
That won't dissolve.

MACBETH
> Will you rest here today?

BANQUO
I must ride on, my lord.

MACBETH
My hope had been to seek your good advice—   20
Which always is both sober and rewarding—
Before the council meets. We'll talk tomorrow.
Will you ride far?

BANQUO
The ride, my lord, will fill up all the time
Until the banquet. Unless my horse moves faster,   25
I'll need to borrow something from the darkness,
Perhaps an hour or two.

MACBETH
> Don't fail to show.

BANQUO
My lord, I will not miss the feast.

MACBETH
I hear our bloody cousins now reside
In England and in Ireland, still denying   30
Their cruel patricide, filling up ears
With crazy tales, but more of that tomorrow
When that and more affairs of state will need
Our joint attention. Get on your horse. Adieu,
Till you return tonight. Will Fleance go too?   35

BANQUO
Yes, my good lord. This is a pressing matter.

MACBETH
I pray that these are swift, sure-footed horses,
And thus I now entrust you to their backs.
Farewell.

[Exit BANQUO]

Each man may use his time as he sees fit   40
Until tonight. To give companionship
A sweeter welcome, let's keep to ourselves
Till supper-time at seven. God be with you!

[Exit all except MACBETH and one SERVANT]

You there, a word with you. Those men—Are they
Still waiting?   45

SERVANT
They are, my lord, outside the palace gate.

MACBETH
Bring them to see me.

[Exit SERVANT]

                    To be king means nothing
Unless I'm safe. My fears concerning Banquo
Are lodged deep, and the kingliness that reigns
His nature should be feared. There's much he'd dare.   50
And the undaunted firmness of his mind
Comes with a wisdom that will guide his valor
To act with caution. There is no one else
Whose mere existence scares me; under him,
My spirit's put to shame, as Caesar did   55
To Antony's. He scolded those three sisters
When they first laid the name of king on me,
And made them speak to him. Then, prophet-like,

They hailed the father of a line of kings.
Upon my head they placed a crown that bears   60
No fruit, and put a barren sceptre in
My grip, wrenched loose by unrelated hands,
No son of mine succeeding me. If so,
It's Banquo's heirs for whom I've ruined my mind;
For them, the grace-filled Duncan I have murdered,   65
Put bitterness in my communion cup—
Only for them—and my immortal jewel,
Delivered to man's foremost enemy,
To make them kings, the seeds of Banquo, kings!
Rather than that, let fate meet me inside   70
The ring and battle to the end!—Who's there?—

[Re-enter the SERVANT, with two ASSASSINS]

[to the SERVANT] Go to the door, and stay there till we
call.

[Exit SERVANT]

Was it just yesterday we spoke together?

BOTH ASSASSINS
Pleasing your highness, yes, it was.[1]

MACBETH
Well then, have you considered my proposal? You know that   75
he's the one who, in the past, has kept your fortunes down,
a circumstance you blamed on innocent me. I proved this
to you in our last discussion, by going over evidence of how
he took you in, how you were thwarted, his tools and how
he worked them, enough for even half-wits or crazed minds   80
to say, "There's no doubt Banquo did this."

FIRST ASSASSIN
You made it clear to us.

MACBETH
I did and then went further, which is why

I called this second meeting. Is it true
That patience is so central to your nature   85
That you can let this go? And do the gospels
Tell you to pray for this man and his sons,
Whose heavy hand has bent you toward the grave
And turned yours into beggars?

FIRST ASSASSIN
We are men, my liege.   90

MACBETH
Indeed, the catalog lists you as men,
As hounds and greyhounds, mongrels, spaniels, curs,
Retrievers, poodles, and half-wolves will all
Receive the label "dog." The breeder's file
Distinguishes the swift, the slow, the sneaky,   95
The guard dog, and the hunter—every one
According to the gift that bounteous nature
Endows it with, which qualifies it for
A title pointing to those special traits
Not common to them all. The same for men.   100
Now, if you have a listing in the file,
That's not among the lowest ranks of men,
Speak out, and I'll place this task in your trust,
Whose execution takes your enemy out,
Straps you securely to the heart and love   105
Of one whose health hangs limply while he lives,
But perfect when he dies.

SECOND ASSASSIN
                         I'm one, my liege,
Whom the vile whacks and wallops of the world
Have so enraged that I'll be reckless in
My quest to spite the world.

FIRST ASSASSIN
                         And I'm another,   110
So weary of disasters, mauled by fortune,
That I would risk my life on any scheme
That betters it or ends it.

MACBETH
                    Both of you
Know Banquo is your enemy.

BOTH ASSASSINS
                         True, my lord.

MACBETH
And he is mine, and in so bloody close,   115
That every minute he exists his thrusts
Come closer to my heart, and though I could
With barefaced power sweep him from my sight
And say my crown allows it, yet I must not
Because of friends that are both his and mine,   120
Whose backing I can't lose. Instead I'll mourn
The fall of one that I struck down. And so
I'm courting your assistance, hoping to
Conceal this business from the public eye
For various weighty reasons.

SECOND ASSASSIN
                              We shall, my lord,   125
Perform what you command.

FIRST ASSASSIN
                         Although our lives....

MACBETH
Your spirit's shining through. Within an hour,
I will advise you where to plant yourselves,
Inform you of the best intelligence[2]
As to the time, for it must be tonight,   130
Some distance from the palace. Make it seem
That I am in the clear. Along with him
(To leave no stains or scratches in this plan)
Fleance, his son, who keeps him company,
Whose exit's no less vital to me than   135
His father's, must embrace the same fate too
In that dark hour. Make up your minds in private.
I'll come and see you soon.

BOTH ASSASSINS
We've made them up, my lord.

MACBETH
I'll call on you at once. Wait just outside.   140

[Exit ASSASSINS]

It is decided. Banquo, your soul's flight,
If it finds heaven, it must be tonight.

[Exit]

Macbeth Instructing the Assassins

Scene Two. Another Room in Forres Castle

[Enter LADY MACBETH and a SERVANT]

LADY MACBETH
Has Banquo left the palace?

SERVANT
Yes, madam, but returns again tonight.

LADY MACBETH
Go tell the king, when he is free, I'd like
A few words with him.

SERVANT
Madam, I will.   5

[Exit]

LADY MACBETH
No gain, all's spent,
When we fulfill desires but aren't content.
It's safer to be that which we destroy,
If with destruction doubts dwell in our joy.

[Enter MACBETH]

Ah, here you are, my lord! Why be alone   10
With only wretched musings for companions,
Pursuing thoughts which should have died with those
That they concern? Things now beyond all remedy
Should be beyond regard. What's done is done.

MACBETH
We've slashed the snake, not killed it.   15
She'll heal, and be herself, and those same fangs
Will threaten our pathetic nastiness.
But let the fabric come apart, let both realms perish,
Rather than eat our meals in fear and sleep

Afflicted by these terrifying dreams   20
That shake us nightly. Better with the dead,
Whom we, for peace of mind, have sent to rest
In peace, than lie here tortured by our minds
In sleepless frenzy. Duncan's in his grave.
After life's fitful fever, he sleeps well.   25
Treason has done its worst. No steel, no poison,
Civil unrest or foreign army, nothing
Can touch him any more.

LADY MACBETH
                    Come noble lord.
Smooth out your wrinkled brow. Be bright and cheerful
Among your guests tonight.

MACBETH
                    I will, my love,   30
And pray that you are too. Remember to
Pay heed to Banquo. Show him favor with
Both eye and tongue. While we're unsafe, we'll rinse
Our honor clean in streams of flattery,
And let our faces mask what's in our hearts,   35
Disguising what they are.

LADY MACBETH
                    You must cease this.
MACBETH
O, full of scorpions is my mind, dear wife!
Remember Banquo, and his son, still live.

LADY MACBETH
But nature's lease on them is not eternal.

MACBETH
There's comfort in that; they are vulnerable.   40
Then you be cheerful. Before the bat has made
It's bell-tower flight, before the sorceress Hecate
Rings in the yawning night with drowsy hums
Of beetles bred in dung, a dreadful deed
Will have been carried out.

LADY MACBETH

What will be done? 45

MACBETH
Stay clear of any guilt, my little chick,
Till you can cheer the deed. Come, blinding night,
Sew shut the eyelids of the caring day
And with your bloody and invisible hand
Cancel and tear to pieces life's great bond 50
Which keeps me pale. Light grows dim, and the crow
Takes wing to rook-filled woods.[3]
The day's good things begin to droop and drowse
While hungry agents of black night carouse.
My words astonish you, but you keep still. 55
We'll strengthen this bad start with greater ill.
Please place your trust in me.

[Exit]

Scene Three. Near Forres Castle

[Enter the two ASSASSINS and a THIRD ASSASSIN]

FIRST ASSASSIN
And who told you to join with us?

THIRD ASSASSIN

Macbeth.

SECOND ASSASSIN
There's no need for mistrust since he can state
The smallest details of our plans and knows
What we must do.

FIRST ASSASSIN
Then wait beside us here.
The west still glimmers with some streaks of day. 5

The lagging traveler's digging in his spurs
To reach the inn on time, and now here comes
The one we're waiting for.

THIRD ASSASSIN
                Hark! I hear horses.

BANQUO
[voice] Give us some light here, ho!

SECOND ASSASSIN
                        He's here. The rest
That are among the list of guests are in   10
The court by now.

FIRST ASSASSIN
                They're off their horses, walking.

THIRD ASSASSIN
The last half mile or so. He always does.
From here up to the palace gate all men
Will lead them in.

SECOND ASSASSIN
                A light, a light!

THIRD ASSASSIN
                      That's him.

FIRST ASSASSIN
Be brave.   15

      [Enter BANQUO and FLEANCE with a torch]

BANQUO
There will be rain tonight.

FIRST ASSASSIN
                Let it come down.

[Attacks BANQUO]

BANQUO
O, treachery! Flee, dear Fleance, flee, flee, flee!
And seek revenge—O villain!

[Dies. FLEANCE escapes.]

THIRD ASSASSIN
Who put the light out?

FIRST ASSASSIN
    Wasn't I supposed to?

THIRD ASSASSIN
There's just one down. His son has fled.

SECOND ASSASSIN
      We've missed 20
The most important one.

FIRST ASSASSIN
    Well, let's go back,
And tell how much we've done.

[Exit]

Scene Four. A Hall in the Castle

[A banquet table is prepared. There are two thrones]

[Enter MACBETH, LADY MACBETH, ROSS, LENNOX,
LORDS, and ATTENDANTS]
[LADY MACBETH sits on one throne]

MACBETH
You know your places, so sit down. For one
And all, a hearty welcome.

LORDS

We thank your majesty.

[They sit]

MACBETH

I'll sit where I can mingle with the guests
And play the humble host.
Our hostess will stay seated, but when time,   5
I'll ask her for her welcome.

LADY MACBETH

Announce it for me, sir, to all our friends,
For my heart says they're welcome.

MACBETH

See, they are toasting you to show their thanks.

[The LORDS toast and bow toward LADY MACBETH]

Both sides are filled. I'll sit here in the middle.   10

[Enter FIRST ASSASSIN at the door]

Be full of mirth. [moves toward the door]
                    Hold on, we'll share a toast
Around the table.—[to the ASSASSIN] There's blood upon
     your face.

FIRST ASSASSIN

It's Banquo's then.

MACBETH

Well, better it's on you than inside him.
Is he dispatched?

FIRST ASSASSIN

                    My lord, his throat is cut.   15
I did him in myself.

MACBETH
                    Then you're the best
Of cutthroats, as is he who did the same
To Fleance. If you're the one, you have no equal.

FIRST ASSASSIN
Most royal sir—Fleance escaped.

MACBETH
[aside] Here comes my pulse again. So close to perfect,   20
As smooth as marble, anchored like a rock,
As free and wild as the surrounding air,
But now I'm closed in, cramped, confined, bound up
By nagging doubts and fears—[to the ASSASSIN] But safe
    from Banquo?

FIRST ASSASSIN
Yes, my good lord. He's safely in a ditch,   25
With twenty gashes hacked into his head,
The least one surely fatal.

MACBETH
                    Thanks for that.
The full-grown snake lies there. The hatchling's fled
Whose nature will in time arm it with venom,
Though it is toothless now. Be gone. Tomorrow   30
We'll speak when we're alone.

                    [Exit FIRST ASSASSIN]

LADY MACBETH
                    My royal lord,
We need a toast. They'll think this is an inn
Unless they're reassured, while they are dining,
That they are welcome. Why not eat at home
If there's no courtesy to add some sauce?   35
A gathering's bland without it.

MACBETH
                    A sweet reminder!—

The best of health to all your appetites—
And stomachs!

LENNOX

        Would his highness care to sit?

        [The GHOST OF BANQUO rises,
        and sits in Macbeth's place]

MACBETH
Beneath one roof we'd have our country's nobles,
Had we been honored with our Banquo's presence,   40
Whom I'd prefer to chide for his lax manners
Than grieve for his misfortune!

ROSS

           His absence, sir,
Makes one suspect his promise. Would your highness
Please grace us with your royal company?

MACBETH
The table's full.

LENNOX

        We saved this place for you, sir.   45

MACBETH
Where?

LENNOX
Here, my good lord. What's troubling your highness?

MACBETH
Which one of you did this?

LORDS

        Did what, my lord?

MACBETH
[to the GHOST] You cannot say I did it. Do not nod
Your gory scalp toward me.   50

ROSS
Gentlemen, rise. His highness is not well.

LADY MACBETH
Sit, worthy friends. My lord will have these spells—
He's had them since his youth. So please, keep seated.
These fits are momentary. In a flash
He'll be himself again. If you make comments,   55
You'll just offend him and prolong his state.
Ignore him and eat on.

            [Takes MACBETH aside]

                Are you a man?

MACBETH
Yes, one who's bold and dares to look at things
That might appall the devil.

LADY MACBETH
                Ridiculous.
You're looking at that portrait of your fear—   60
That dagger in the air— the one, you said,
Led you to Duncan. O, these fits and bursts,
When matched against real fear, are suited for
Some woman's yarn told by a winter fire
And vouched for by her grandma. Shame on you!   65
Why do you make such faces? After all,
It's just an empty chair.

MACBETH
Oh, please. Right there! Look! Now what do you say?
[to the GHOST] What do I care? If you can nod, then
    speak.—
If catacombs and graveyards want to send   70
All those we bury back, our resting place
Will be a buzzard's stomach.

        [The GHOST of BANQUO disappears]

LADY MACBETH
Has folly made you meek?

MACBETH
As sure as I stand here, I saw him.

LADY MACBETH
                                        Shameful.

MACBETH
Blood has been shed before, in olden times,   75
Before humane laws pacified our realm.
And after that some murders were performed
Too brutal for our ears. There was a time,
When brains fell out, the man would surely die,
And that was it. But now they rise again,   80
With twenty lethal lesions on their head,
And push us off our chairs. This shakes us more
Than any murder could.

LADY MACBETH
                              My worthy lord,
Your noble friends now need you.

MACBETH
                              Yes, I forgot—
[to the GUESTS] Don't look at me amazed, my worthy
      friends.   85
I have a strange affliction, nothing new
To those who know me. Come, love and health to all.
Now, I'll sit down.—And fill this full of wine.—
Here's to the common joy of all those present,
And to my dear friend Banquo, whom I miss   90
And wish were here! To you and him, I drink,
Each man to every man.

LORDS
                        And here's to you.

[The GHOST of BANQUO rises again]

MACBETH
Away, and leave my sight! Let the earth hide you!
Your bones are marrowless, your blood is cold;
There's no perception left in those two eyes   95
With which you glare!

LADY MACBETH
                        Don't think of this, good friends,
As more than just his way. It's nothing more;
It spoils our pleasure only for a moment.

MACBETH
What man dares, I dare.
Come at me like some rugged Russian bear,   100
An armored rhino, or an Asian tiger;
Take any form but this, and these firm limbs
Will never tremble. In some deserted place,
Come back to life and dare me with your sword.
If trembling dwells here still, proclaim that I'm   105
A dolly for some girl. Go, horrible shadow!
You unreal mocker, go!

[The GHOST OF BANQUO disappears]

                        Why...now it's gone,
I am a man again.—Please, take your seats.

LADY MACBETH
You've ousted mirth and order from this gathering
With this astounding tantrum.

MACBETH
                        Can such things be   110
And pass us over like a summer cloud
Attracting no real interest? You make me seem
A stranger even to my usual self,

When I see you can look upon such sights
And keep the natural ruby of your cheeks,   115
When mine are bleached with fear.

ROSS
                    What sights, my lord?

LADY MACBETH
Please do not speak. It only makes him worse.

The Ghost of Banquo

Questions enrage him. So a quick good night.
Ignore the order of your rank when leaving.
Just go at once.

LENNOX
Good night. May better health   120
Await his majesty!

LADY MACBETH
A kind good-night to all!

[Exit all LORDS and ATENDANTS]

MACBETH
It will want blood, they say. Blood will want blood.
Stones have been known to move, and trees to speak.
Prophecies made, and evidence revealed   125
By magpies, crows, and rooks have brought to light
The bloody hand best hidden.—How late is it?

LADY MACBETH
Soon night will yield to morning, I suppose.

MACBETH
And what about Macduff refusing to
Appear before me.

LADY MACBETH
Did you send for him?   130

MACBETH
I heard it indirectly, but I will.
There's not a house in which I do not have
A servant in my pay. I'll go tomorrow
And make an early call on those weird sisters.
They'll tell me more, for I intend to know,   135
By wicked means, the worst. For me to win,
All other things must yield. The blood I'm in
Is now so deep that heading back to shore,
Will be as tough as wading into more.

Strange thoughts insist they move from head to hand,   140
And carried out before they can be scanned.

LADY MACBETH
You're lacking what preserves existence—sleep.

MACBETH
Yes, let's sleep now. More practice should reduce
These fears that fill my head—this strange abuse.
We're new to this indeed.   145

[Exit]

Scene Five. The Heath

[Thunder. Enter the three WITCHES, meeting
HECATE]

FIRST WITCH
Why, Hecate, it is you. And you look angry.

HECATE
And for good reason, hags, as you're aware.
Impertinent and too bold, how did you dare
To trade and traffic with Macbeth
In riddles and affairs of death,   5
And I, the mistress of your charms,
The secret schemer of all harms,
Was never called to play my part,
Or show the glory of our art?
And, even worse, all you have done   10
Is merely for some perverse son—
Spiteful and wrathful—who, as others do,
Cares for his own gain, not for you.
But make amends now and be gone,
And at the pit of Acheron   15

Tomorrow morning you and he
Will come to know his destiny.
Bring bottles, cauldrons, every spell,
Your charms, and everything as well.
I'll join the air. The night I'll spend   20
Achieving a disastrous, fatal end.
Our great work must be done by noon.
Upon the corner of the moon
A drop whose properties astound,
I'll catch before it hits the ground.   25
That drop, distilled by magic rites,
Will raise up such deceitful sprites,
That, through the strength of their illusion,
He'll be drawn to his confusion.
He'll spurn his fate, scorn death, and steer   30
His hopes past prudence, luck, and fear.
And you all know, complacency
Is mortals' biggest enemy.

[Music and song are heard, "Come away, come away
Hecate, Hecate, oh come away"][4]

Hark! I am called. My little spirit, see,
Sits in a foggy cloud and waits for me.   35

[Exit]

FIRST WITCH
Come, let's be quick. She'll soon be back again.

[Exit all]

Scene Six. A Room in a Palace

[Enter LENNOX and another LORD]

LENNOX
My earlier words are in line with your thoughts,
So draw your own conclusions. I will say this—
There've been strange goings-on. The "godly" Duncan
Was pitied by Macbeth—once he was dead—
The ever valiant Banquo, out too late   5
Was killed by Fleance, as one might suppose,
Since Fleance fled. Men must not be out late.
Who can't help thinking what a monstrous deed
It was for Malcolm and for Donalbain
To kill their godly father? Damn this crime!   10
And how it grieved Macbeth! Did he not slash,
At once in loyal rage, two criminals
Enslaved by drink and in the bonds of sleep?
Was that not nobly done? Yes, and wisely too,
For it would anger any heart alive,   15
To hear those men deny it. So I would say,
He's managed all this well, and I do think,
If Duncan's sons were in his custody
(As heaven has it, they are not), they'd find
What killing fathers means—and so would Fleance.   20
Enough. From such blunt talk and failure to
Appear at this usurper's feast, I hear
Macduff is out of favor. Can you say
Where he has taken refuge?

LORD
                         Duncan's son,
Whose birthright's kept from him by this usurper,   25
Lives in the English court and is received
By pious Edward with such favor that
Malevolent misfortune can't reduce
The great esteem for him. It's there Macduff,
On his behalf, now heads to ask the holy king,   30
To wake Northumberland and warlike Siward
So that with help from them (with God above

To sanction this campaign) we may again
Have on our tables meat, sleep in our nights,
Our feasts and banquets free of bloody knives,   35
Show true allegiance, earn our honors freely,
All things we yearn for now. And news of this
Exasperates the king so much that he
Is now preparing for a war.[5]

LENNOX
Did he send for Macduff?   40

LORD
He did, and with an absolute "Sir, not I,"
The scowling messenger then turned his back
With a "harrumph," as if to say "You'll rue
The time spent on this answer."

LENNOX
                          He might do well
To show some sense and use his head to keep   45
At some safe distance. And some holy angel
Could fly to England's court ahead of him
And give his message so that a swift blessing
Can soon return to this, our suffering country,
Held under an accurséd hand.   50

LORD
I'll send my prayers with him.

[Exit]

Macbeth

Act Four

Act Four

Scene One. A Dark Cave with a Cauldron

[Thunder. Enter the three WITCHES]

FIRST WITCH
Thrice the banded cat's meowed.

SECOND WITCH
Thrice, and once the hedge-hog whined.

THIRD WITCH
The harpy cries "It's time, it's time.

FIRST WITCH
Round and round, you cauldron, spin;
Throw the poisoned entrails in.   5
Toads, that under cold stone lay,
Thirty nights and one more day
Till the sweated venom's got,
Boil it first in this charmed pot!

ALL THREE
Double, double, toil and trouble;   10
Fire burn, and cauldron bubble.

SECOND WITCH
Fillet of swamp-bred snake,
In the caldron boil and bake.
Eye of newt, and toe of frog,
Wool of bat, and tongue of dog,   15
Adder's fork, and blind-worm's sting,

89

Lizard's leg, and owlet's wing,—
For a brew of powerful trouble,
Like a hell-broth boil and bubble.

ALL
Double, double, toil and trouble;   20
Fire burn, and cauldron bubble.

THIRD WITCH
Scale of dragon, tooth of mutt,
Witch's mummy, jaw and gut
Of the salty, ravenous shark,
Root of hemlock dug in dark,   25
Spleen of unbelieving Jew,
Gall of goat, and twigs of yew
Sliced off in the moon's eclipse,
Nose of Turk, and Tartar's lips,
Finger from a fetus which   30
Whores left stillborn in a ditch,
Make the gruel as thick as pitch.
Then we add a tiger's colon,
To the mixture in our cauldron.

ALL
Double, double, toil and trouble;   35
Fire burn, and cauldron bubble.

SECOND WITCH
Cool it with a báboon's blood,
Then the hex is fixed and good.

[Enter HECATE with three of her WITCHES]

HECATE
O, well done! I commend your pains,
And everyone will share the gains.   40
And now around the cauldron sing,
Like elves and fairies in a ring,
Enchanting all that you put in.

ALL

> Song: Black Spirits
> *Black spirits and white*
> *Red spirits and gray;*   45
> *Mingle, mingle, mingle*
> *You that mingle may.*

[Exit HECATE and her three WITCHES]

> *Around, around, about, about*
> *The bad run in, the good keep out.*[1]

SECOND WITCH

There's a tingling in my thumbs.   50
Something wicked this way comes.
Open, locks, whoever knocks!

[Enter MACBETH]

MACBETH

What's this, you secret, spooky, midnight hags?
What are you doing?

ALL THREE

> A deed without a name.

MACBETH

I call on you and all you claim to know   55
(No matter how you learned it)—answer me.
Though you unleash the winds and let them fight
Against the steeples, though the frothy waves
Destroy and swallow up armadas whole,
Though ripened corn's knocked flat and trees blown down, 60
Though castles topple on their masters' heads,
Though tops of palaces and pyramids
Collapse on their foundations, though the seed
All nature springs from tumbles all at once
Till devastation sickens of itself,   65
I need an answer.

FIRST WITCH
Speak.

SECOND WITCH
Demand.

THIRD WITCH
We'll answer.

FIRST WITCH
Say if you'd rather hear it from our mouths,
Or from our masters?

MACBETH
Call them, let me see them.

FIRST WITCH
Pour in sow's blood, one that's eaten
Her nine offspring; grease that's beaten   70
From a murderer's carcass—fling
Upon the flame.

ALL THREE
From far or near
You and your function now appear!

[Thunder. The first APPARITION,
a helmeted head, rises]

MACBETH
Tell me, you unknown power....

FIRST WITCH
He knows your thoughts.
Hear his speech, but do not speak.   75

FIRST APPARITION
Macbeth! Macbeth! Macbeth! Beware Macduff.
Beware the Thane of Fife. Dismiss me. Enough.

[The APPARITION descends]

MACBETH
Whatever you are, I thank you for this warning.
My fears pluck those same strings. But one word more—

FIRST WITCH
He will not be commanded. Here's another   80
More potent than the first.

[Thunder. The second APPARITION,
a bloody child, rises]

SECOND APPARITION
Macbeth! Macbeth! Macbeth!

MACBETH
Had I three ears, I'd listen.

SECOND APPARITION
Be bloody, bold, and resolute. And scorn
The power of man: no one of woman born   85
Shall harm Macbeth.

[The APPARITION descends]

MACBETH
Then live, Macduff, for why should I fear you?
Yet I'll make this assurance double sure,
And make fate's contract binding. If you don't live,
Then I can call the bloodless heart of fear   90
A liar and sleep through thunder.

[Thunder. The third APPARITION, a crowned child with
a tree in his hand, rises]

                              —What is this?
It rises like the offspring of a king,
And wears upon his baby brow the crown
And hat of sovereigns.

ALL THREE
Listen, but don't speak to it.   95

THIRD APPARITION
Be lion-tough, be proud, and give no thought
To those who stew, who fret, or where they plot.
Macbeth cannot be vanquished, not until
Great Birnam wood can climb Dunsinane hill
To rise against him.

                    [the APPARITION descends]

MACBETH
                    That will never be.   100
Who can recruit a forest, have a tree
Pull up its earth-bound roots? Sweet omens, good!
Rebellious dead will not rise till the wood
Of Birnam rises, and high-ranked Macbeth
Will live out nature's lease, spend his last breath   105
As time and custom has it. Yet my heart
Throbs to know one thing. Tell me, if your arts
Can tell so much: Will Banquo's offspring ever
Reign in this kingdom?

ALL THREE
                    Seek to know no more.

MACBETH
I must be satisfied. Deny me this,   110
And you will be eternally cursed! Yes, I must know!

            [The cauldron sinks. Hautboys are heard]

Why is the cauldron sinking? What's this sound?

FIRST WITCH
Show him!

SECOND WITCH
Show him!

THIRD WITCH
Show him!   115

ALL THREE
Show his eyes, make his heart grieve.
Come as shadows, shadows leave!

[Eight KINGS appear, and pass by in order, the last one,
    has a crystal ball in his hand. BANQUO follows them]

MACBETH
You're too much like the spirit of Banquo. Down!
Your crown, it sears my eyeballs. And your hair,
This second gold-laced brow is like the first.   120
The third is like the former.—Filthy hags!
Why do you show me this?—A fourth!—Eyes, burst!
What? Will this line stretch on till judgment day?
Another still? A seventh? I'll look no more.
And still an eighth appears, who holds a ball   125
Which shows me many more, and some I see
Are carrying double balls and triple scepters.
Horrible sight!—Now I see it's true,
For this blood-matted Banquo smiles at me,
And gestures that they're his. —Can this be so?   130

FIRST WITCH[2]
Ay, sir, all this is so:—but why's
Macbeth now showing such surprise?
Let's raise his spirit to new heights,
And show the best of our delights;
I'll charm the air to give us sound,   135
While you bizarrely dance around;
So this great king may kindly say
That we appreciate his stay.

[Music. The WITCHES dance and then vanish]

MACBETH
Where are they? Gone?—Let this malicious hour

Be cursed forever in the calendar—   140
Come in. Who's out there?

[Enter LENNOX]

LENNOX

Your grace, what do you want?

MACBETH
Did you see three weird sisters?

LENNOX

No, my lord.

MACBETH
They did not pass you?

LENNOX

No indeed, my lord.

MACBETH
Infected is the air through which they fly,
And all who trust them damned!—I know I heard   145
The galloping of horses. Who rode by?

LENNOX
There's two or three, my lord, to tell you that
Macduff has fled to England.

MACBETH

Fled to England?

LENNOX
Yes, my good lord.

MACBETH
[Aside] Time, you anticipate my dreadful moves.   150
The fleeting purpose will not be achieved
Unless I act at once. From this time on,
Whatever's firstborn in my heart shall be

What's firstborn in my hand. And starting now,
I'll crown my thoughts with acts—if thought, it's done.   155
The castle of Macduff I will surprise;
I will seize Fife and lay against my sword
His wife, his babes, and all unfortunate souls
That follow in his line. No boasting like mere fools.
This deed I'll do before this purpose cools.   160
But no more visions! [Aloud] Where are these gentlemen?
Come, show me where they are.

[Exit]

Scene Two. A Room in Macduff's Castle

[Enter LADY MACDUFF, MACDUFF's
SON, and ROSS]

LADY MACDUFF
What did he do that's made him flee the land?

ROSS
You must remain composed, madam.

LADY MACDUFF
                              Did he?
To run was foolish. When our actions don't,
Our fears still make us traitors.

ROSS
                              You don't know
Whether it was from prudence or from fear.   5

LADY MACDUFF
Prudence? To leave his wife, to leave his babes,
His mansion, and his titles, in a place
From which he flees? He could not love us much.

He lacks the natural itch. The tiny wren,
The most diminutive of birds, will guard   10
The young ones in her nest against an owl.
All this is fear, and none of it is love.
There's little prudence when to flee from this
Runs hard against all reason.

ROSS
                    My dearest coz,
You must control yourself. As for your husband,   15
He's noble, wise, judicious, and knows best
What fits the season. I dare not say much more,
But these are cruel times when we are traitors
And yet don't know we are; when we judge rumors
By what we fear, yet don't know what we fear,   20
But float upon a wild and violent sea
And move this way and that—I must leave now.
It won't be long before I'm back again.
Things at their worst will either cease or climb
To what they were before.—[to MACDUFF'S SON] My
    handsome cousin,   25
You have my blessing!

LADY MACDUFF
He has a father, yet he's fatherless.

ROSS
I'm such a fool that if I stayed here longer,
I would disgrace myself and cause distress.
I'll leave at once.

                    [Exit]

LADY MACDUFF
                    Young man, your father's dead.   30
And what will you do now? How will you live?

MACDUFF'S SON
As birds do, mother.

LADY MACDUFF
What, on worms and flies?

MACDUFF'S SON
On what I catch, I mean; that's what they do.

LADY MACDUFF
Poor bird! You'd never spot the net or pit,
The sticky trap or snare.   35

MACDUFF'S SON
Why should I, mother? It's not poor birds they're set for.
My father is not dead, as you have said.

LADY MACDUFF
No, he is dead. Now who will be your father?

MACDUFF'S SON
And who will be your husband?

LADY MACDUFF
Why, I can buy me twenty at any market.   40

MACDUFF'S SON
That means you plan to sell them too.

LADY MACDUFF
It must take all your brain to think such things
And yet it's quite a lot.

MACDUFF'S SON
Is my father a traitor, mother?

LADY MACDUFF
Yes, he is.   45

MACDUFF'S SON
What is a traitor?

LADY MACDUFF
Why, one that swears an oath and lies.

MACDUFF'S SON
And do all traitors do that?

LADY MACDUFF
Everyone that does so is a traitor and must be hanged.

MACDUFF'S SON
Must everyone be hanged who swears and lies?   50

LADY MACDUFF
Every one.

MACDUFF'S SON
Who must hang them?

LADY MACDUFF
Why, the honest men.

MACDUFF'S SON
Then the liars and swearers are fools, for there are liars and
swearers enough to beat the honest men and hang them.   55

LADY MACDUFF
Now, God help you, poor monkey! Who will be your father?

MACDUFF'S SON
If he were dead, you'd weep for him. If you do not, it is a
good sign that I will soon have a new father.

LADY MACDUFF
You chatterbox, how you talk!

[Enter a MESSENGER]

MESSENGER
Bless you, fair dame! I am not known to you,   60
Though I know well that you're of noble rank.

I dread some danger soon will come your way.
If you will take a simple man's advice,
Do not stay here. Leave, with your little ones.
To frighten you like this seems cruel to me;   65
To do more harm would be a deadly act,
Which now seems all too near. Heaven preserve you!
I can remain no longer.

[Exit]

LADY MACDUFF
                  Where can I flee?
I've done no harm. But I remember now
I'm in a dirty world, where to do harm   70
Is often laudable, where good sometimes
Is thought a dangerous folly. Why do I then
Alas, put up that womanish defense
And say I've done no harm?—What are these faces?

[Enter ASSASSINS]

FIRST ASSASSIN
Where is your husband?   75

LADY MACDUFF
I hope in no place so unsanctified
That types like you could find him.

FIRST ASSASSIN
                      He's a traitor.

MACDUFF'S SON
You lie, you shag-haired villain!

FIRST ASSASSIN
                  What, you shrimp?

[Stabs him]

You traitor's runt, you!

MACDUFF'S SON
                    He is killing me.
Run, mother, run. I beg you! [Dies]   80

[Exit LADY MACDUFF, crying "Murder," pursued by
the ASSASSINS who carry off MACDUFF'S SON]

Scene Three. England. Outside the King's Palace

[Enter MALCOLM and MACDUFF]

MALCOLM
Let's find a vacant piece of shade and weep
Till our sad hearts are empty.

MACDUFF
                    Let's clutch instead
Our deadly swords, and like good men, stand up
Above our fallen birthright. Each new dawn,
New widows howl, new orphans cry, new sorrows   5
Slap heaven in the face, which then resounds
As if it feels with Scotland, roaring back
Each syllable of anguish.

MALCOLM
When I believe, I'll cry.
When proven, I'll believe. And when I can,   10
I'll take the time to redress all I can.
What you have said, it may be so perhaps.
This tyrant, whose mere name now blisters tongues,
Was seen as upright and admired by you.
He has not touched you yet. I'm young but sense   15
I may be used to get to him. It's smart
To offer up a weak, poor, innocent lamb
When you appease an angry god.

MACDUFF
I am not treacherous.

MALCOLM
               But Macbeth is.
When loaded with a king's command we may   20
Recoil from good and virtue. Do not take this wrong.
Your nature can't be altered by my thoughts.
Angels still shine although the brightest fell.
All wicked things wear virtue on their brow,
Yet virtue still looks good.

MACDUFF
               I've lost all hope.   25

MALCOLM
And that is why my own suspicions grew.
Why would you leave your family so exposed—
Strong knots of love are grounds enough to stay—
With no good-bye? Now, please, these doubts are not
About your honor—see them as concerns   30
For my own safety. Your action may be just,
Regardless of my thoughts.

MACDUFF
                  Bleed, bleed, poor country!
Great tyranny, go lay a strong foundation—
The good won't dare object! Fly your crimes high,
Your claim is uncontested.—Fare well, lord: 35
I would not be the villain you describe
For all the land that's in this tyrant's grasp
And all the Eastern riches.

MALCOLM
               Don't be offended.
This is not from complete mistrust of you.
I know our country sinks beneath the yoke.   40
It weeps, it bleeds, and each new day a gash
Is added to her wounds. I also know

That many hands would join to back my claim,
And England's gracious king has made a pledge
Of many thousands. Yet with all this,   45
Once I have tread upon the tyrant's head,
Or wear it on my sword, still my poor country
Will have more vices than it had before
Will suffer more, and in more ways than ever,
From he who has the throne.

MACDUFF
                        Who would this be?   50

MALCOLM
I mean myself, for I know I am one
In whom all sorts of vices have been grafted
So much that when they flower, black Macbeth
Will seem as pure as snow, and this poor state
Will see him as a lamb, when judged against   55
The widespread harm I'll bring.

MACDUFF
                       In all the legions
Of horrid hell no devil damned for evil
Could ever top Macbeth.

MALCOLM
                   It's true he's bloody,
And lecherous, avaricious, false, deceitful,
Reckless, malicious, smacks of every sin   60
That has a name. But there's no bottom, none,
To my lasciviousness. Your wives, your daughters,
Your matrons, and your maids, could not fill up
The cistern of my lust, and my desire
Would overwhelm all barriers the chaste   65
Put up against me. Better it's Macbeth
Who reigns than one like this.

MACDUFF
                  Boundless indulgence
Can be a tyrant too, and it has caused

The quick demise of many happy thrones
And many kings to fall. Still do not fear   70
To take back what is yours. You can partake
Of these abundant pleasures secretly
Yet still seem chaste and fool the world at large.
With all these willing dames, you cannot be
A vulture who'd devour more than those   75
Who'd sacrifice themselves to satisfy
A great one so inclined.

MALCOLM
                       And there would grow
From my too wicked disposition such
A ravenous avarice that, were I king,
I'd cut the nobles down to get their lands,   80
Want this man's jewels, while taking this one's house.
And having more would be a sauce to make
Me hunger more, so much that I would forge
False barbs and aim them at the good and loyal,
Destroying them for their wealth.

MACDUFF
                         This avarice   85
Is lodged much deeper with more toxic roots
Than summer-season lust, and it has been
The sword that's slain our kings. Yet do not fret.
Scotland is rich and you have wealth enough
To keep you full. The cost is bearable   90
When weighed against your virtues.

MALCOLM
But I have none of these: the kingly virtues,
Like truth and justice, temperance, steadiness,
Charity, perseverance, mercy, meekness,
Devotion, patience, courage, fortitude.   95
I have no trace of them, but overflow
With variations that I can perform
On every type of crime. If I had power, I would
Pour the sweet milk of harmony on hell,

Demolish universal peace, destroy   100
All unity on earth.

MACDUFF
        O Scotland, Scotland!

MALCOLM
If such a man is fit to govern, speak.
I'm everything I told you.

MACDUFF
        Fit to govern?
Not fit to live!—O nation miserable,
With a usurping tyrant's bloody scepter,   105
When will you see your wholesome days again,
Now that the most deserving of your throne
Disqualifies himself and stands in shame
Before his parentage?—Your royal father
Was a most holy king; the queen that bore you,   110
More often on her knees than on her feet,
Would pray like each day were her last. Fare well!
These evils you recount against yourself
Have banished me from Scotland.—O dear heart,
Your hope ends here!

MALCOLM
        Macduff, these noble feelings,   115
Born of integrity, have wiped these dark
Suspicions from my soul, convinced my mind
That you are true and worthy. Devilish Macbeth
With many schemes like this has sought to trick
Me to return, and prudence plucks me back   120
From a too-credulous haste. But God above
Will lead us in our dealings! For even now
I will accept your guidance and withdraw
My self-recrimination and denounce
The stains and blame I laid upon myself   125
As strangers to my being. I have yet
To know a woman or to break a promise,
Barely desire the things that I now own,

Have always kept my faith, would not betray
The devil to his comrade, and delight   130
In truth as much as life. My first false words
Were those about myself. So truly I
Am yours and my poor country's to command—
Where, to be sure, before your coming here,
Old Siward, with ten thousand well-armed men   135
Already standing by, was on the march.
Now we'll unite and hope our chances are
As good as our just cause! Why are you silent?

MACDUFF
Such welcome and unwelcome things at once
Are hard to reconcile.   140

[Enter a DOCTOR]

MALCOLM
More later.—Tell me, is the king up yet?

DOCTOR
Yes, sir. A crowd of wretched souls await
His healing touch. Their maladies defeat
The greatest of my cures, but with his touch—
The holiness that heaven gives his hand—   145
Restores them instantly.

MALCOLM
                                I thank you, Doctor.

[Exit DOCTOR]

MACDUFF
And what is this disease?

MALCOLM
                                It's called "The Evil."
The good king's work is quite miraculous,
Which I have often seen since coming here
To England. Only he knows how he calls   150

On heaven's help, but those with strange afflictions,
Inflamed and ulcerous, pitiful to see,
Beyond the help of surgeons, he will cure,
Hanging a golden coin around their necks,
Placed there with holy prayers; and it is said   155
He'll leave to royalty succeeding him
This healing power. Along with this strange talent,
The king has heaven's gift of prophecy,
And other blessings hang around his throne
That show he's full of grace.

MACDUFF
                              Ah, look who's here.   160

MALCOLM
A fellow Scot, but I do not know who.

                    [Enter ROSS]

MACDUFF
My ever-noble cousin, welcome, welcome.

MALCOLM
I recognize him. God will soon remove
The things that make us strangers!

ROSS
                              Sir, amen.

MACDUFF
Is Scotland still the same?

ROSS
                    Alas, poor country,   165
Almost afraid to look upon itself!
It's not our mother—it's our grave, where nothing
Will smile unless it has known nothing else;
Where sighs and groans and shrieks rip through the air
Without remark; where violent sorrow seems   170
A routine feeling. Bells ring for the dead

But few will now ask who, and good men's lives
End faster than the flowers in their caps,
Dying before they're ill.

MACDUFF
                O, nicely stated
And yet too true!

MALCOLM
                What is the latest grief?   175

ROSS
One that's an hour old brings only hisses.
Each minute teems with new ones.

MACDUFF
                How's my wife?

ROSS
Why, peaceful.

MACDUFF
And my children?

ROSS
The same.   180

MACDUFF
Their peace has not been battered by the tyrant?

ROSS
No, they were quite at peace when I last saw them.

MACDUFF
You're stingy with your news. What's going on?

ROSS
When I came here to bring to you the tidings,
Which I have sadly done, there was a rumor   185
Of many worthy fellows up in arms,

Which in my mind became more credible
When I observed the tyrant's troops were out.
It's time for help. [to MALCOLM] Your eyes alone in Scotland
Would rally soldiers, make our women fight   190
To shed their dire distress.

MALCOLM
                         They'll cheer up when
They learn we're coming. Gracious England has
Lent us ten thousand men, led by good Siward,
The best, most seasoned soldier to be found
In all the Christian world.

ROSS
                         I wish that I   195
Could add more cheerful news! But I have words
That should be howled out in the desert air
Where ears aren't there to hear them.

MACDUFF
                              Concerning what?
A matter for us all? Or grief whose fee
Is paid by just one heart?

ROSS
                         An honest mind   200
Would have to share the cost, though most the woe
Pertains to you alone.

MACDUFF
                    If it is mine,
Don't keep it from me. Quickly let me have it.

ROSS
Don't let your ears despise my tongue forever,
Which now will be possessed by heavier sounds   205
Than they have ever heard.

MACDUFF
                    Unhh! Don't make me guess.

ROSS
Your castle was attacked, your wife and babes
Savagely slaughtered. To relate the manner
Would only serve to add you to the pile
Of murdered dear ones.

MALCOLM
                              Merciful heaven!—   210
Talk, man! Don't ever hold your hat in sorrow.
Use words. The whispers of unspoken grief
Will overload a heart, not bring relief.

MACDUFF
My children too?

ROSS
                    Wife, children, servants, all
That could be found.

MACDUFF
                         I had to be away!   215
My wife killed too?

ROSS
                    I'm sorry.

MALCOLM
                         Let's find a cure
By making medicines for our revenge,
To treat this deadly grief.

MACDUFF
He has no children.—All my pretty ones?
Did you say all?—O, buzzards from hell!—All?   220
What, all my pretty chickens and their hen
In one fell swoop?

MALCOLM
                    Then fight back like a man.

MACDUFF
O, I'll do that,
But I must also feel it as a man.
I cannot help but think of things that were,   225
Most precious to me.—Could heaven look on this
And then not join their side? Sinful Macduff,
You let them be struck down! For wickedness—
Not theirs, not something they deserved, but mine—
Souls cruelly slaughtered. Heaven let them rest.   230

MALCOLM
Make this the whetstone for your sword. Let grief
Convert to anger. Don't blunt your heart; enrage it.

MACDUFF
I know my eyes could play the woman's part,
My tongue the braggart's role!—But, gentle heavens,
Cut short the passing time and bring this fiend   235
Of Scotland here to meet me face to face
Within a sword's length. If this brute escapes,
Heaven forgive him too!

MALCOLM
                         This tune sounds manly.
Come, we'll go see the king. Our army's ready;
His leave's the only thing we lack. Macbeth's   240
So ripe he'll drop when shook. The powers above
Are well-equipped. So take what comfort comes your way.
The night is long that never seeks the day.

[Exit]

Macbeth

Act Five

Act Five

[Enter a medical DOCTOR and a GENTLEWOMAN]

DOCTOR (serving Lady Macbeth)
I have stayed up two nights with you but cannot verify what
you report. When did she last walk in her sleep?

GENTLEWOMAN (serving Lady Macbeth)
Since his majesty left for the battlefield, I have seen her rise
from her bed, throw on her robe, unlock her cabinet, take
out paper, write on it, read it, fold it, then seal it up, and go   5
back to bed, yet do all this while in a very deep sleep.

DOCTOR
Quite abnormal behavior—to receive at once the benefit
of sleep and give the appearance of waking. During this
sleepy activity, besides walking and performing other actions, what, at any time, have you heard her say?   10

GENTLEWOMAN
Things, sir, which I don't want to report about her.

DOCTOR
You may to me, and it's quite proper that you do.

GENTLEWOMAN
Not to you or any one else, not without a witness to confirm
what I say.

[Enter LADY MACBETH, with a candle]

115

Lo and behold, here she comes! This is the exact same   15
behavior, and, heaven help me, fast asleep. Observe her.
Stay hidden.

DOCTOR
Where did she get the candle?

GENTLEWOMAN
Why, she keeps it by her. It's continually lit. She insists
on it.   20

DOCTOR
Look, her eyes are open.

GENTLEWOMAN
Yes, but shut to any sensation.

DOCTOR
What is she doing now? Look how she rubs her hands.

GENTLEWOMAN
It is a customary action with her, to pretend she's washing
her hands. I have seen her continue like this for a quarter   25
of an hour.

LADY MACBETH
There's still a spot.

DOCTOR
Listen, she's speaking. I will write down what comes from
her, to assure that my memory is accurate.

LADY MACBETH
Out, damned spot! Out, I say! [as if hearing a bell chime]   30
One, two. Why, then it's time to do it. Hell is dark! Shame
on you, my lord, shame! A soldier, and afraid? Why fear
those who know it when no one has the power to charge
us?[1]—Yet who would have thought the old man would have
so much blood in him?   35

DOCTOR
Did you catch that?

LADY MACBETH
The Thane of Fife had a wife. Where is she now? What, will these hands never be clean? No more of that, my lord, no more of that. Your flinching spoils everything.

DOCTOR
It's true. You do know things that you should not.   40

GENTLEWOMAN
She has said things that she shouldn't, I am sure of that. Heaven knows what she knows.

LADY MACBETH
There's still the smell of blood. All the perfumes of Arabia will not sweeten this little hand. Oh, oh, oh!

DOCTOR
What a sigh that is! Her heart is terribly burdened.   45

GENTLEWOMAN
I would not have such a heart in my bosom for all the majesty a body could have.

DOCTOR
Well, well, well,—

GENTLEWOMAN
God be well, sir.

DOCTOR
This disease is beyond my skills. Those I know who walked   50
in their sleep died a holy death in their beds.

LADY MACBETH
Wash your hands. Put on your robe. Don't look so pale—I'll tell you once again, Banquo's buried; he can't come out of his grave.

DOCTOR
Could it be?   55

LADY MACBETH
To bed, to bed. There's knocking at the gate. Come, come,
come, come. Give me your hand. What's done cannot be
undone. To bed, to bed, to bed.

[Exit]

DOCTOR
Will she go to bed now?

GENTLEWOMAN
Immediately.   60

DOCTOR
Foul rumors everywhere. Unnatural deeds
Will breed unnatural trouble. Infected minds
Reveal to their deaf pillows secret crimes.
She needs divine help more than a physician.
God, God, forgive us all. Look after her.   65
Remove from her all means to harm herself,
And keep an eye on her. So now, good night.
She's stupefied my mind and stunned my sight.
I think, but dare not speak.

GENTLEWOMAN
                                            Good night, good doctor.

[Exit]

Scene Two. The Countryside near Dunsinane

[MENTEITH, CAITHNESS, ANGUS, LENNOX, and
SOLDIERS enter with drummers and flag-bearers]

MENTEITH (a Nobleman)
The English troops are near, led on by Malcolm,

His uncle Siward, and the good Macduff.
They're burning with revenge, for their dire cause
Prompts men on their last legs to hear the call
And join the flowing blood.

ANGUS (a Nobleman)
                              Near Birnam wood   5
We'll no doubt meet them. That's the way they're coming.

CAITHNESS (a Nobleman)
Who knows if Donalbain is with his brother?

LENNOX
It's certain, sir, he's not. I have a list
Of all the gentry. There is Siward's son
And many smooth-faced youths, who soon will get   10
The first test of their manhood.

MENTEITH
                              Where's the tyrant?

CAITHNESS
He's strongly fortifying Dunsinane.
Some say he's mad; others, who hate him less,
Will call it valiant fury. But, it's certain—
The belt he rules with is too short to reach   15
Around his bloated cause.

ANGUS
                              So now he feels
His secret murders sticking on his hands.
His breach of faith now brings revolts each minute.
Those he commands move only in command,
Not out of love. And now he feels how loose   20
His title hangs on him, a giant's robe
Upon a dwarfish thief.

MENTEITH
                              And no surpise
If his beleaguered senses flinch and wince

When all that is within his mind condemns
Itself for being there.

CAITHNESS
                Well, let's march on,   25
To give obedience where it's truly owed.
To join up with the cure for our sick state,
And with him pour out every drop to flush
Our country clean.

LENNOX
                Or as much as we need
To feed the sovereign flowers and drown this weed.   30
Now let's march on towards Birnam.

              [Exit, marching]

Scene Three. Dunsinane. In Macbeth's Castle

    [Enter MACBETH, DOCTOR, and ATTENDANTS]

MACBETH
Bring me no more reports. Let them desert.
Till Birnam wood climbs up to Dunsinane,
Fear can't pollute me. Who is this boy Malcolm?
Was he not born of woman? The spirits that know
The fate of every mortal told me this: 5
"Fear not, Macbeth; no man that's born of woman
Will ever overpower you." Flee, turncoat thanes,
And mingle with your English dinner guests.
The mind that rules me, and this heart that's here,
Will never sag with doubt nor shake with fear.   10

        [Enter a SERVANT]

The devil turn you black, you paste-faced loon!
Why look like such a goose?

SERVANT

                     There are ten thousand—

MACBETH
Geese, scoundrel?

SERVANT
Soldiers, sir.

MACBETH
Go prick your face and coat your fear with red,   15
You lily-livered boy. What soldiers, clown?
Death to your soul! Those linen cheeks of yours
Are advocating fear. What soldiers, milk-face?

SERVANT
The English force, sir.

MACBETH
Get your face out.

            [Exit SERVANT]

            Seyton!—I'm sick at heart,   20
When I behold—Seyton, I say!—This thrust
Props up my throne for good or knocks me off.
I have lived long enough. My life, its path
Is withering in the fall, a yellow leaf,
And things that should accompany old age,   25
Like honor, love, obedience, hordes of friends,
I can't expect to have, but in their place,
Curses, not loud but deep, lip-service, words
My poor heart should ignore but doesn't dare to.
Seyton!—   30

            [Enter SEYTON]

SEYTON (Attendant to Macbeth)
What does your grace desire?

MACBETH
          Any news?

SEYTON
All the reports, my lord, are now confirmed.

MACBETH
I'll fight until they hack off all my flesh.
Give me my armor.

SEYTON
       It's not needed yet.

MACBETH
I'll put it on.   35
Send out more horsemen, scour the countryside.
Hang those that talk of fear. Give me my armor.
How is your patient, doctor?

DOCTOR
Not that sick, my lord.
It's these delusions coming hard and fast   40
That keep her from her rest.

MACBETH
              Cure her of that.
Why can't you cure a mind that is diseased,
Pluck from her memory deep-rooted sorrow,
Erase the troubles written in the brain,
And with some sweet obliterating drug   45
Free her clogged bosom of the perilous stuff
That weighs upon her heart?

DOCTOR
              That kind of patient
Must cure herself.

MACBETH
Throw medicine to the dogs. I'm through with it.
Come, put my armor on. Give me my staff.   50

Send someone for it.—The Thanes are fleeing, doctor.
Go quickly, sir.—If you could, doctor, take
A water sample, find what ails this land,
And purge it back to sound and perfect health,
I would applaud until I hear its echo   55
Applaud you once again.—[to SEYTON who is dressing him]
    Pull this, I say.—
[to the DOCTOR] What rhubarb stalk, what herb, what
    cleansing drug,
Would flush these English out? Heard anything?

DOCTOR
Yes, my good lord. The castle's mobilized,
And it hears something.

MACBETH
                          Bring my gear along.   60
I'll feel no danger to my life and reign,
Till Birnam forest comes to Dunsinane.

[Exit all except the DOCTOR]

DOCTOR
If Dunsinane were far away from me,
You could not draw me there for any fee.

[Exit]

Scene Four. A Forest near Dunsinane

[Enter, with drum and flag-bearers, MALCOLM, SI-
WARD and YOUNG SIWARD, MACDUFF, MENTEITH,
CAITHNESS, ANGUS, LENNOX, ROSS, and SOL-
DIERS, marching]

MALCOLM
Cousins, I hope the days are near at hand
When beds are safe again.

MENTEITH

                  We do not doubt it.

SIWARD
What is this forest called?

MENTEITH

                  It's Birnam Wood.

MALCOLM
Have every soldier cut himself a branch,
And carry it in front of him to mask   5
Our army's numbers so that their observers
Will err in their reports.

SOLDIERS

                It shall be done.

SIWARD (Commander of the English Forces)
We know just this: the overconfident tyrant
Is staying put in Dunsinane, and will
Allow us to lay siege.

MALCOLM

                It's his main hope;   10
For where there's opportunity to flee,
Both noblemen and commoners desert,
And those who serve are little more than captives
Whose hearts are absent too.

MACDUFF

                Hold all appraisals
Until the outcome's known and focus on   15
The work of soldiering.

SIWARD

                The time approaches
When we with more exactness can assess
What we have lost and what we still possess.

Our doubts and hopes prompt us to speculate
But certain issues blows must arbitrate.   20
Command the army to advance.

[Exit, marching]

Scene Five. Dunsinane. In Macbeth's Castle

[Enter with drum and colors, MACBETH,
SEYTON, and SOLDIERS]

MACBETH
Hang out our banners on the outward walls.
The cry's still, "Let them come." Our castle's strength
Will make their siege a joke. We'll let them camp
Till famine and diseases eat them up.
If they weren't reinforced by those who left,   5
We'd meet them in the open, beard to beard,
And drive them back home beaten.

[The sound of women crying]

What's that noise?

SEYTON
The women—they are crying, my good lord.

[SEYTON exits]

MACBETH
I barely can recall the taste of fear.
There was a time my senses would run cold   10
To hear a shriek at night; my scalp and hair
Would rise and stir at any dreadful tale
As if I'd lived it. I'm stuffed full of horrors.
Ghastliness, made a friend by murderous thoughts,
Could never rattle me.

[Re-enter SEYTON]

Why all this crying?   15

SEYTON
The queen, my lord, is dead.

MACBETH
Her death should have been after this.[2]
There would have been a time to hear such words.
Tomorrow, and tomorrow, and tomorrow,
Creeps in this petty pace from day to day,   20
To the last syllable of recorded time,
And all our yesterdays have lit for fools
The way to dusty death. Out, out, brief candle!
Life's but a walking shadow, a poor player
Who struts and frets his hour upon the stage,   25
And then is heard no more. It is a tale
Told by an idiot, full of sound and fury,
Signifying nothing.

[Enter a MESSENGER]

You're here to use your tongue—your message quickly.

MESSENGER
My gracious lord,   30
I should report to you all that I saw,
But know not how to do it.

MACBETH
                    Well, speak, sir.

MESSENGER
As I stood at my watch upon the hill,
I looked toward Birnam, and it seemed to me
The woods began to move.

MACBETH
                    Liar and slave!   35

[Striking him]

MESSENGER
I will endure your wrath if it's not so.

You'll see it coming less than three miles off.
I'm sure, a moving grove.

MACBETH
                If you are wrong,
I'll hang you from the nearest tree alive
Till famine shrinks you. If this talk is true,   40
I won't care if you do the same to me.
I'm pulling on the reins of my resolve,
Now wise to these equivocating fiends
Who lie with truth. "Fear not, till Birnam woods
Climbs up to Dunsinane," and now the woods   45
Come here to Dunsinane.—Prepare to fight—
If what he has asserted does appear,
We cannot flee nor can we tarry here.
I'm starting to grow weary of the sun
And wish the world's creation were undone.—   50
Go ring the call to arms!—Blow, wind! World, crack!
At least we'll die with armor on our back.

                [Exit]

Scene Six. A Plain Outside Macbeth's Castle

    [MALCOLM, SIWARD, MACDUFF, and others, with
          drum and flags, enter with their army,
              carrying branches]

MALCOLM
We're close enough. Throw down your leafy cover,
And show them who you are.—You, worthy uncle,
Will with my cousin, your most noble son,
Lead First Battalion. Your King and brave Macduff
Will take care of what else there is to do   5
According to our plans.

SIWARD
              And then fare well.

If we can meet the tyrant's force tonight,
Let us be beaten, if we cannot fight.

MACDUFF
Make all our trumpets sound—with all your breath—
A deafening alarm of blood and death.   10

[Exit]

Scene Seven. A Battlefield near Macbeth's Castle

[Trumpets sound. Enter MACBETH]

MACBETH
They've tied me to a stake. I cannot flee,
But, like a bear, must fight the pack. Who's he
Who was not born of woman? Such a one
Am I to fear, or none.

[Enter YOUNG SIWARD]

YOUNG SIWARD (Siward's Son)
What is your name?

MACBETH
                    You'll be afraid to hear it.   5

YOUNG SIWARD
Not even if you have a hotter name
Than any that's in hell.

MACBETH
                    My name's Macbeth.

YOUNG SIWARD
The devil himself could not announce a name
More hateful to my ear.

MACBETH
                    No, nor more feared.

YOUNG SIWARD
You lie, abhorrent tyrant. With my sword   10
I'll test this lie you speak.

[They fight, and YOUNG SIWARD is slain]

MACBETH
                    You're born of woman.—
And swords I smile at, weapons are a joke,
When brandished by a man of woman born.

[Exit]
[Trumpets sound. Enter MACDUFF]

MACDUFF
Here's where the noise is.—Tyrant, show your face!
If you are slain and if the stroke's not mine,   15
My wife and children's ghosts will haunt me still.
I can't strike wretched infantry, whose arms
Are hired to carry spears. It's you, Macbeth,
Or it's my sword, with an unbattered edge,
That I must sheathe unused. [Trumpets sound] That must
    be you.   20
With such commotion, one of highest rank
Is being announced. With any luck I'll find him!
And no more do I ask.

[Exit. Trumpets sound]
[Enter MALCOLM and SIWARD]

SIWARD
This way, my lord. The castle gave up quickly,
The tyrant's troops are fighting on both sides,   25
The noble thanes showed courage in the war,
The day itself has almost joined with you,
And little's left to do.

MALCOLM
                    Some of our foes
Now fight beside us.

SIWARD
                    Enter, sir, the castle.

[Exit. Trumpets sound]

Scene Eight. Another Part of the Battlefield

[Enter MACBETH]

MACBETH
I'm not some foolish Roman general
Who dies by his own sword. While others live,
The gashes suit them better.

[Enter MACDUFF]

MACDUFF
                    Turn, hell-hound, turn!

MACBETH
Of all men I've avoided you the most.
But you stand back. My soul's already burdened   5
With too much of your blood.

MACDUFF
                         I have no words—
My voice is in my sword. You're bloodier, villain,
Than language can describe!

[They fight]

MACBETH
                    Your effort's futile.
It's easier to cut shapes out of air
With your sharp weapon than to make me bleed.   10
Slash at the plumes on vulnerable helmets;
My life is charmed and must not yield to one
Who's born of woman.

MACDUFF
> Forget this faith in charms
And make the demon you have always served
Say this: Macduff was ripped out early from   15
His mother's womb.

MACBETH
A curse upon the tongue that tells me this,
For it has cowed the better part of me!
And place trust in these scheming fiends no more
Who baffle us with all their double meanings   20
Who keep the promise that we hear but in
A sense that crushes hope!—I will not fight you.

MACDUFF
Then yield you coward,
And be the main attraction of our time
And like our more unusual freaks, we'll hang   25
Your picture on a pole, and write beneath
"Come in and see the tyrant."

MACBETH
> I will not yield,
To kiss the ground beneath young Malcolm's feet,
And be the bait that draws the rabble's curse.
Though Birnam Wood has come to Dunsinane,   30
And my opponent's not of woman born,
Yet I will still test fate. In front of me
I throw my warrior's shield. Strike hard, Macduff,
And damn the one who first cries out, "Enough!"

[Exit fighting]
[Trumpets sound]

[They re-enter, fighting. MACBETH is slain.
MACDUFF removes the body]

Scene Nine. Nearby on the Battlefield

[Trumpets sound. Enter, with drum and flag-bearers, MALCOLM, SIWARD, ROSS, LENNOX, ANGUS, CAITHNESS, MENTEITH, and SOLDIERS]

MALCOLM
I wish the friends we lost were here unharmed.

SIWARD
Some must depart and yet from these I see,
The greatness of this day was cheaply bought.

MALCOLM
Macduff is missing, and your noble son.

ROSS
[to SIWARD] Your son, my lord, has paid a soldier's debt. 5
He only lived until he was a man—
His gallantry too soon put to the test
When he unshrinking stood his ground and fought—
But like a man he died.

SIWARD
                                    Then he is dead?

ROSS
Ay, sir, we brought him back. Your grounds for sorrow   10
Must not be measured by his worth, for it
Would have no end.

SIWARD
                                    Were his wounds from behind?

ROSS
No, in the front.

SIWARD
                          Why then, he is God's soldier!
Had I as many sons as I have hairs,
I could not wish for them a finer death.   15
So ring the bell for him.

MALCOLM
                                    He's worth more sorrow,
Which I will save for him.

SIWARD
                                    No worthier praise.
They say he left us bravely, his duty done.
So, God be with him!—Here's something we can cheer.

[Enter MACDUFF, with Macbeth's head on a pole]

MACDUFF
Hail, king, indeed. Behold the curséd head   20
Of our usurper. Freedom in our time.
You are surrounded by your kingdom's pearls
Who in their minds deliver this salute,
Whose voices I hope speak aloud with mine.
Hail, King of Scotland!   25

ALL
Hail, King of Scotland!

[Trumpets sound]

MALCOLM
I won't invest a large amount of time
Before I recognize the love you've shown
And even our account. My thanes and kinsmen,
From now on you are earls, to be the first   30
That Scotland's honored with that name. There's more
That we must plant at once in this new time,
By calling home our exiled friends abroad,
Who fled the snares of meddling tyranny,
And bringing forth the brutal ministers   35
Of this dead butcher and his fiendish queen—
Who, it is thought, with her own violent hand
Took her own life—this, and whatever else
Demanded of us, by the grace of grace,
We'll finish at the proper time and place.   40
I thank you all at once and each alone,
Whom I invite to see me crowned at Scone.

[Trumpets sound. Exit]

The End

Endnotes

Act One

[1] The meter in the Captain's report has irregularities that I preserved. I assume the officer is trying to give a formal report, but his condition makes it difficult.

[2] Scholars disagree on whether the original " 'gins its reflection" refers to the sun rising in the east or returning north as spring approaches.

[3] Editors have tried unsuccessfully to get Duncan's question and the officer's response to scan as blank verse. I treated Duncan's line as prose. The officer's reply has long and short lines, which I preserved.

[4] Apparently Macbeth does not realize that he defeated the treasonous Thane of Cawdor and that the thane has been sentenced to death. Samuel Johnson felt that Macbeth's ignorance was improbable, but we can assume that Macbeth was a battlefield commander too busy and absorbed in the battle with the Norwegian king to realize all that he had accomplished.

[5] The original reads, "His wonders and his praises do contend/Which should be thine or his." Every editor seems to have a different longwinded paraphrase of what this phrase might mean.

[6] The dispute here concerns whether the line should read "Thick as hail" or "Thick as tale." The latter would supposedly mean "rapidly counted" with tale linked etymologically to the current word tally.

[7] The original phrase "my single state of man" has no agreed upon meaning. Both the meaning of *single* and *state of man* are disputed. Some say *single* means "weak" or "feeble."

Others suggest "unified" or "undivided" or perhaps "unconflicted."

[8] Since Shakespeare's original word *assassination* is commonplace today, why did I substitute the murkier word *dispatching* (Macbeth uses *dispatch* later in the play)? The word *assassination* was most likely coined by Shakespeare from the noun *assassin* for a one-time use in this play. Shakespeare clearly wanted Macbeth to employ a self-conscious euphemism to avoid the more disturbing word *murder.* Today the word *assassination* is no longer euphemistic, so ironically Macbeth is too well understood by modern audiences. Incidentally, according to the *Oxford English Dictionary*, the verb *assassinate* does not appear in print until 1618, two years after Shakespeare's death.

[9] The dispute concerns the *First Folio*'s "Banke and Schoole." Some scholars argue that the phrase means "bench" (as in judicial bench) and "school." This reading ties the image to the judicial and pedagogical references in the lines that follow. One objection to the aquatic reading is the redundancy of "bank and shoal" since both could refer to sand or sandbars. But Shakespeare often employed closely related pairs of words to fill out the meter or clarify the sense ("slings and arrows").

[10] The original is "But screw your courage to the sticking place." English teachers love this line because it is an example of a conceit. Yet scholars are not sure about the underlying metaphor. Is the "sticking place" a notch that holds a taut string in place on a musical instrument or crossbow? Or does it mean tightening a screw until it turns no more, tightening the strings on a musical instrument, or winding up the cord on a crossbow? Or is the sticking place a point beyond which a moral individual will not go?

Act Two

[1] The original line reads "To know my deed, 'twere best not know myself." The interpretations divide roughly into two camps. (1) To think about this murder, I must not think about the man I once was. (2) If I think clearly, I would recognize what I have done, so it is best to be lost in thought (or even lose consciousness). Here are several alternate translations that scan.

> Clear thinking means I must not think of me.
> Reflection means reflecting on myself.
> If I must think, I'd best not think of me.

Act Three

[1] Editors have tried various ways to force the murderers' response and Macbeth's rationalization for murder into iambic pentameter lines, but in all cases the meter becomes ragged, the line breaks are odd, and some lines are clearly unmetrical. A. R. Braunmiller, Robert S. Miola, and Stanley Wells all favor a prose reading in their editions. My translation is iambic but dispenses with the pentameter line breaks.

[2] The original is the mysterious, "Acquaint you with the perfect spy o'th'time." Samuel Johnson says that "perfect spy" refers to the third murderer or some other informant. Some say this is unlikely because these two murderers seem surprised when they meet the third in Act 3, Scene 3. However, because it is getting dark, they may be simply checking him out. Most settle for a meaning on the order of "spying out the most favorable time [to carry out the plan]." This reading may accord better with Act 3, Scene 3, but the syntax of "with the perfect spy o'th'time" makes that interpretation suspicious as well. Is Macbeth instructing them to figure out the best time or is he promising to find out the best time? I decided he was promising. Here are translations for the other senses.

> Acquaint you with a well-placed spy who knows
> The perfect time....

> Determine for yourselves with careful spying
> The perfect time....

[3] There are meter problems in the original lines.

[4] The *Oxford Shakespeare* includes an additional 33 lines that fill out the song sung by the spirits. Other editions, typically in the appendix, commentary or textual notes, include one of several versions from Thomas Middleton's play *The Witch*, from William Davenant's musical adaptation of Macbeth (1674), or from a compilation of the two. For productions that prefer a longer song, here's a translation that combines elements of Middleton's and Davenant's versions.

Song in the Air

FIRST SPIRIT
Come away, come away. Hecate, Hecate.
Oh, come away.

[spirits lower from the sky]

HECATE
I come, I come, I come, I come,
With all the speed I may,
With all the speed I may,
Where's Staddle.

SECOND SPIRIT
Here.

HECAT
Where's Puckle?

THIRD SPIRIT
Here.
And Hopper and Hellway too.
We just lack you, we just lack you.
Come away, and fill the skies.

HECATE
I'll grease myself and then I'll rise.
I'll grease myself and then I'll rise.

FIRST SPIRIT
Here comes one to fetch his dues,
A kiss, a hug, a sip of blood,
Why do you wait so long, I muse.
Since the air's so sweet and good.

HECATE
O, have you come?
What news, what news?

SECOND SPIRIT
All goes well to our delight.
Either come, or else refuse, refuse.

HECATE
Now I'm ready for the flight.
Now I go, and now I fly,
Malkin, my sweet cat, and I.

THIRD SPIRIT
O, what a tasty pleasure this.
To sail the air while the moon shines fair.
To sing, to flirt, to dance, and kiss.

A CHORUS OF SPIRITS
Over woods, high rocks, and mountains,
Over hills and misty mountains,
Over steeples, towers, and turrets,
We fly by night in troops of spirits!
No ringing bells to our ear sounds,
No noisy wolves nor yelping hounds
No breakers crashing in the night
Nor cannon growls can reach this height.

[5] Scholars cannot agree on whether "the king" refers to Macbeth or King Edward. I have left it ambiguous. Lennox's next line suggests that Macbeth is preparing for war, but Macbeth's later surprise at hearing news of Macduff's actions complicates this interpretation.

Act Four

[1] The *Oxford Shakespeare* includes a 15-line version of the song, gleaned from Thomas Middleton's play *The Witch*, where the witches add more ingredients to the cauldron. Hecate remains on stage. G. K. Hunter feels only a couple of lines are necessary for the purposes of this play. I favor that view and include only the opening and closing lines of Middleton's version. For productions that prefer a longer song, here's a translation that combines elements of Middleton's text and a version in William Davenant's adaptation of *Macbeth* (1674).

FOURTH WITCH
Kitty Tiffin, add it stiff in,
Firedragon muck to give it luck,
Lying Robin, you must bob in.

CHORUS OF WITCHES
Around, around, about, about
The bad run in, the good keep out.

FIFTH WITCH
Here's the blood of a bat.

FOURTH WITCH
                    Put in that, O, put in that.

SIXTH WITCH
Here's lizard's brain.

FOURTH WITCH
                    Put in a grain.

FIFTH WITCH
Here's juice of toad, here's oil of adder
Those will make the spell grow madder!

FOURTH WITCH
Put all it in and raise a stench.

SIXTH WITCH
Yes, here's three ounces of the red-haired wench.

[2] In editions where Hecate remains on stage, Hecate has these lines. Most scholars agree that Shakespeare did not write them.

Act Five

[1] The *Folio* punctuation breaks up this sentence into two questions. "What need we fear? Who knows it, when none can call our power to accompt?" Most editors favor the more straightforward single question. I accepted that change to avoid the wordy paraphrase "Why do we need to fear anything? Who could know the truth when no one has the power to charge us?"

[2] Editors note the ambiguity of the original "She should have died hereafter." The two most common interpretations are "It would have been better if she had died at a later time" (allowing time to honor her properly) or "She would have died anyway."

Appendix 1: How Iambic Pentameter Works

With the exception of the *Merry Wives of Windsor*, which is 90% prose, Shakespeare's plays employ generous servings of a verse line known as iambic pentameter. Some of his early plays are almost entirely in this form, and all but four plays are at least 50% verse. So it is useful to understand something of iambic pentameter in order to develop an ear for its complex rhythms and to appreciate its dramatic uses.

The term iambic pentameter has three parts which together give a rough description of this verse form. The term *meter* refers to a pattern of rhythm. If you pronounce most two-syllable words in a natural way, you will sense a rhythm, with one syllable receiving more energy than the other. Say the words in (1) and note the different rhythms:

(1)   táble (stressed/unstressed)
        prefér (unstressed/stressed)

An accent mark over a vowel indicates that the syllable containing that vowel is pronounced with more energy than the syllable without the accent mark. We call this increased energy "stress," and an accented syllable is called a stressed syllable. Syllables with less energy are called "unstressed."

Iambic refers to a pattern of meter where an unstressed syllable precedes a stressed syllable. The words in (2) have an iambic rhythm and each forms a metrical unit known as an *iamb*:

(2)   affórd, forbíd, inféct, adópt

Two-word sequences can also have an iambic rhythm.

(3)   a bít, the mán, to gó, is mád, of míne

The term **penta** (five) tells us how many instances of this iambic rhythm make up a line. Each instance is traditionally called a **foot**, so an iambic pentameter line has five iambic feet, or **iambs**. In these ten-syllable lines of five iambs (4), observe how the even-numbered syllables get more stress than the odd numbered syllables.

(4)   Thy gláss/ will shów/ thee hów/ thy béau/ties wéar/
      1   2   3   4   5 6   7 8   9   10
                                       (Sonnet 77, line 1)
      And cáll/ upón/ my sóul/ withín/ the hóuse/
      1   2   3 4   5 6   7 8   9 10
                                (Twelfth Night, 1.5.251)
      Beshréw/ that héart/ that mákes/ my héart/ to gróan/
      1 2   3   4   5   6   7   8   9 10
                                   (Sonnet 133, line 1)

We sense that the 2nd, 4th, 6th, 8th, and 10th syllables (marked with ´) receive more emphasis than the 1st, 3rd, 5th, 7th, and 9th syllables. In (5), the line has ten syllables, but notice that it is not iambic pentameter. If we use the jargon of verse analysis, we say the line does not **scan**.

(5)   Récog/níze the/ rhýthm's/ nót i/ámbic/
      1 2   3   4   5 6   7 8 9 10

Here the 1st, 3rd, 5th, 7th, and 9th syllables receive the emphasis. If we placed this line after any of the lines in (4), we would not sense a meter developing and would interpret the passage as prose.

(6)   Thy gláss/ will shów/ thee hów/ thy béau/ties wéar/
      Récog/níze the/ rhýthm's/ nót i/ámbic/

One appealing feature of iambic pentameter is that it sounds like verse yet seems natural. The perfectly iambic lines in (7) were randomly selected from different plays. Read them in sequence and notice how they sound rhythmical without seeming "sing-songy" or bouncy.

(7)   Expóse/ thysélf/ to féel/ what wrétch/es féel/
(King Lear, 3.4.39)
In wóm/en's wáx/en héarts/ to sét/ their fórms/
(Twelfth Night, 2.2.30)
To bréathe/ such vóws/ as lóv/ers úse/ to swéar/
(Romeo and Juliet, 2. Prologue. 10)

The three lines, though not sing-songy, do sound rhythmically monotonous. Imagine a play with 2500 such lines pounding away one after the other. The effect would surely be deadening, and dramatists would be severely limited in the kinds of sentences they could write and the vocabulary they could use. So they relax the rules a bit. Most of these deviations fall into two categories: adding extra syllables and altering the iambic meter.

Adding Extra Syllables

There are three common ways to increase the number of syllables beyond ten.

Feminine Endings
    If every line had to end with an iamb, many, if not most, two syllable words—*mother, pantry, person, hungry*—could never end a line. So iambic lines allow an extra unstressed eleventh syllable (even a twelfth) at the end of line. This eleventh syllable is called a ***feminine ending***, and about 10% of the lines in Shakespeare's early plays and about 30% in his later plays have such endings. The lines from (4) have been modified to show how the feminine ending sounds.

(8) Thy gláss/ will shów/ thee hów/ thy béau/ties wéath*er*/.
     1 2   3   4   5 6   7 8 9   10 Ø
    And cáll upón my sóul withín the pán*try*/
    Beshréw that héart that mákes my héart to súf*fer*/

The words *weather, pantry,* and *suffer* provide the 10th and 11th syllables in these lines, but because the 11th is unstressed, the lines still sound iambic to the trained ear. If feminine endings are allowed, then almost any word can be worked into the end of an iambic pentameter line. In fact, we can easily make the unmetrical line (5) acceptable if we add a syllable at the beginning of the line to push the stressed syllables into the even-numbered positions. Since the 11th syllable is unstressed, it counts as a feminine ending.

(9) *And* réc/ogníze/ the rhýth/m's nót/ iámbic/
       1   2   3 4   5   6   7   8 9 10 Ø

Even without the 11th syllable, adding an extra beat to start the line can restore an iambic rhythm, as *Oh* does here.

(10) Oh, how/ thy worth/ with man/ners may/ I sing/
       (Sonnet 39, line 1)

Syllable Deletions
    Lines can also have extra syllables if a syllable can be dropped without the word becoming unintelligible or sounding unnatural. Note how many three-syllable words can become two-syllable words in rapid or slightly slurred speech.

(11)   interest (intrist)   Goneril (gonril)
       monument (mon^{y}ment)   Romeo (romyo)
       traveler (travler)   Juliet (Julyet)
       Viola (vyola)   valiant (valyent)

The trick in "scanning" Shakespeare is to anticipate whether he intends such words to be two or three syllables. My translations of Shakespeare into contemporary English allow such slurring (traditionally called **syncope**). I do, however, avoid slurrings that seem awkward, incomprehensible, or archaic to modern speakers such as *to't* (to it), *e'en* (even), *show'th* (showeth), *upon't* (upon it), and *lov'st* (lovest).

Epic Caesura
    Lines can have an extra unstressed syllable right before a major punctuation break, a variation called **epic caesura** ("says you're a..."). Note in (12) that the second syllable of the word *kingdom* is unstressed and precedes a major punctuation break. This extra eleventh syllable is not added to the syllable count, creating a mid-line feminine ending of sorts.

(12)   Know that we have divided
In three/ our king/**dom**; and 'tis/ our fast/ intent/
  1   2   3   4   Ø   5   6   7   8   9 10
(King Lear, 1.1.39-40)

    If we allow a feminine ending, slurring, and epic caesura in a single line, we can produce a fairly complex line that stays within the rules of iambic pentameter. How would you scan this thirteen-syllable line (13) from *Twelfth Night*? Is it iambic pentameter?

(13) Even in a minute. So full of shapes is fancy
(Twelfth Night, 1.1.14)

Some scholars question the meter of this line, but here's a try at scanning it. *Even* is slurred to *E'en*. The second, unstressed syllable of *minute* is not counted because it precedes a major punctuation break (epic caesura), and the second, unstressed syllable of *fancy* is a feminine ending.

(14) E'en in/ a min/ute. So full/ of shapes/ is fancy/
       1   2   3   4   Ø   5 6   7   8   9 10 Ø

Shakespeare is pushing the limits here, especially for contemporary speakers who have trouble slurring *even* to *e'en*, but the line technically qualifies as iambic pentameter.

Altering the Meter

Besides an iambic rhythm, a two-syllable foot can have three other rhythms, as shown in the table. These rhythms can be worked into an iambic pentameter line in various ways.

Type of Foot	Rhythm	Single Words	Word Sequences
Trochee	stressed/ unstressed	néver, óffer báttle, únder	whát a, wánt to dróp it
Spondee	stressed/ stressed	cúpcáke súitcáse úpkéep	bád lúck tálks bíg
Pyrrhic Foot	unstressed/ unstressed	suit<u>able</u> hap<u>pily</u> list<u>ening</u>	of a, to it, of the

Spondees

 A spondaic foot—one where both syllables are likely to be stressed—can occur anywhere. Spondees work at the beginning of a line as these revisions of the lines from (4) show.

 (15) ***Bíll's gláss*/** will shów/ thee hów/ thy béau/ties wéar/
   ***Cáll nów*/** upón/ my sóul/ withín/ the hóuse/
   ***Cúrse nót*/** that héart/ that mákes/ my héart/ to gróan/

In (16), spondees (in boldface) are worked into the middle and end of lines.

 (16) Thy gláss/ will shów/ **Bíll hów/** thy béau/ties wéar/
   Upón/ my sóul/ withín/ the hóuse,/ ***cáll nów*/**
   Beshréw/ that héart/ that mákes/ ***Bób's héart*/** to gróan/

Spondees have an interesting effect: they slow down the line. Speakers need time to give stressed syllables extra energy, so lines filled with spondees have a deliberate, pounding rhythm. A line from *King Lear* demonstrates this clearly.

 (17) Nó, nó,/ nó, nó!/ Cóme, lét's/ awáy/ to príson/
              (King Lear, 5.3.9)

Trochees

If every iambic pentameter line had to begin with an iamb, then most English words could not start a line. Yet a quick look at Shakespeare's sonnets reveals a different reality. We find these poems start with stressed one-syllable words (*look, when, not, but, let, lord, how, why, full, take, sin, thus, love*), and trochaic two-syllable words (*béing, wéary, músic, Cúpid*)—all words or phrases that start off the line with a stressed syllable.

Iambic pentameter solves this problem by allowing a trochaic rhythm to start a line. These modified versions of (4) are all acceptable iambic pentameter lines.

(18)   ***Mírrors*/** will shów/ thee hów/ thy béau/ties wéar/
***Cálling*/** upón/ my sóul/ withín/ the hóuse/
***Cúrsing*/** that héart/ that mákes/ my héart/ to gróan/

Trochees can also occur in the middle of a line if they follow a strongly stressed syllable or a major punctuation break In (19), *haply* has a trochaic rhythm, but it is allowed because it follows a major punctuation break. It also follows the heavily stressed word *all*.

(19)   They lóve/ you áll?/ ***Háply*/**, when I/ shall wéd/
(*King Lear, 1.1.110*)

Phrases that appear to be trochaic are permitted if they fall within a lengthy sequence of one-syllable words. In the 3rd foot of (20), we would normally expect the word *love* to get more emphasis than *which*, yielding the trochaic rhythm *lóve, which*.

(20)   A bróth/er's déad/ ***lóve, which*/** she would/ kéep frésh/
(*Twelfth Night, 1.1.30*)

This reading sounds like prose. But notice that the word *which* is surrounded by one-syllable words. In this environment, rarely-stressed words such as *the, which, of, is,* and *been* can be stressed to preserve an iambic rhythm without sounding unnatural, as in (21).

(21)   A bróth/er's déad/ love, whích/ she wóuld/ keep frésh/

Actors may choose not to give the line an iambic rhythm, but the fact that they can qualifies the line as iambic pentameter.

Pyrrhic Feet

Normally, pyrrhic feet do not cause a problem. A foot with two unstressed syllables glides right by without upsetting the meter. The lines in (22) show typical uses of pyrrhic feet (in bold italics).

(22)   For she/ did speak/ in starts/ distract/***edly***/
She loves/ me sure./ The cun/***ning of***/ her passion/
Invites/ in me/ this chur/lish mes/***senger***. /
                          (Twelfth Night, 2.2.20-22)

Unmetrical Lines

If trochaic, spondaic, and pyrrhic feet can come anywhere in a line, then wouldn't just about any ten-syllable line be iambic pentameter? Actually, the meter is more restricted than it appears because of one rule: a word with a trochaic rhythm cannot fill the 2nd, 3rd, 4th, or 5th foot unless a stressed syllable or a major punctuation break precedes that foot. Sounds complicated, but that is the rule violated by the italicized sequence in (23).

(23)   Áft***er***/ ***dínner***/ he wálked/ acróss/ the stréet/
           1 2   3 4   5 6   7 8   9 10

The *-ter* of *after* and the first syllable of the trochaic word *dínner* cannot be in two separate feet because that leaves the stressed syllable of *dinner* in an odd-numbered position surrounded by two unstressed syllables. Forcing the two-syllable word *dinner* into an iambic rhythm is too unnatural, something on the order of *d'nér*. To fix this line, we need to force the first syllable of *dinner* into an even-numbered position. Here are several possibilities.

(24) He áft/er dín/ner wálked/ acróss/ the róad/
       He wálked/ 'cross th' róad/ right áf/ter dín/ner, sír/

The second line requires two elisions—*'cross* and *th' road*. My translations avoid odd-looking elisions like *th' road,* but be ready for them if you delve into the original. Can you figure out these? *Woo't, 'a, s', to't, tak'n, sev'n, within's.* (Answers: *wouldst thou, he, his, to it, taken, seven, within this*).

Regardless of what precedes it, we rarely find a word with a trochaic rhythm filling the last foot. Line (25), like (23), is unmetrical and interpreted as prose, not verse.

(25) He wálked/ acróss/ the róad/ to éat /**dínner**/

Line (25) can be corrected if we force a feminine ending by adding an extra syllable, in this case the word *his*.

(26) He wálked/ acróss/ the róad/to éat/his dínner/
       1   2   3 4   5 6   7 8   9 10 Ø

To highlight the difference between verse and prose, let's mechanically divide a prose passage from *King Lear* into ten-syllable lines. Even with slurring and long lines, only the lines in **bold italics** seem acceptable iambic pentameter, and some of these require uncharacteristic and rather clumsy breaks in the syntax at the end of lines. The other lines all deviate from Shakespeare's usual verse.

(27) **EDMUND**
       This is the exc'llent fopp'ry of the world
       That, when we are sick in fortune—often
       The surfeit of our own behaviour—we
       Make guilty of our disasters the sun,
       The moon, and the stars; as if we were villains
       On necessity; fools by heavenly

Compulsion; knaves, thieves, and treachers by spherical
Pre-dominance; drunkards, liars, and adulterers
By an enforcéd obedience of
Planetary influence; and all that
We are evil in, by a divine thrusting
On: an admirable evasion of whoremaster
Man, to lay his goatish disposition
To the charge of a star! My father compounded
With my mother under the dragon's tail
And my nativity was under Ursa
Major; so that it follows I am rough
And lecherous.—Tut! I should have been that
I am, had the maidenliest star in
The firmament twinkled on my bastardizing.

(King Lear, 1.2.125-140)

All told, only five out of twenty lines can be read as verse, and that is why Edmund's speech is always formatted as prose.

Let's compare Edmund's prose soliloquy to a passage that certainly complicates the iambic pattern yet is always formatted as verse. I have highlighted with ***bold italics*** some of the more difficult lines to scan.

(27) **LEAR**
Peace, Kent!
Come not between the dragon and his wrath.
I lov'd her most, and thought to set my rest
On her kind nursery—Hence, and avoid my sight!
So be my grave my peace, as here I give
Her father's heart from her!—Call France—who stirs?
Call Burgundy!—Cornwall and Albany,
With my two daughters' dowers digest this third:
      [*dowers* is slurred to one-syllable]
Let pride, which she calls plainness, marry her.
I do invest you jointly in my power,
Pre-eminence, and all the large effects
That troop with majesty.—Ourself, by monthly course,
      [long line]
With reservation of an hundred knights,

By you to be sustain'd, shall our abode
Make with you by due turns. *Only we still retain* [long]
The name, and all th' additions to a king;
The sway, revénue, execution of the rest, [long]
Belovéd sons, be yours; which to confirm,
This coronet part betwixt you....[*coronet* slurred]

KENT

Royal Lear,
(King Lear, 1.1.135-155)

This passage is about as wild as Shakespeare's iambic pentameter gets, yet only five of the eighteen lines are difficult to scan. Three are long lines (hexameters), more frequent in Shakespeare's later plays, and the other two deviant lines have rather complicated rhythms, perhaps to signal that Lear is yelling and losing his temper. The last line is an example of a **shared line** where one speaker finishes the line by responding to or overlapping the previous speaker.

This comparison shows that iambic pentameter is not prose and that verse dramatists are quite aware when they are shifting between verse and prose (even if many modern actors obscure the difference). It also shows that iambic pentameter, while it allows for deviation in line length and rhythm, imposes constraints on a line. My translations honor these constraints and aim to preserve in contemporary English the rhythm of Shakespeare's verse.

Scanning Exercise

Here is the untranslated version of Duke Orsino's famous opening speech in *Twelfth Night*. Scholars have argued that the meter is as fickle and impulsive as the Duke himself, with smooth, flowing phrases interrupted by spondaic rhythms.

Try scanning it. You should find at least one example of all the metrical variations described above. I have added several stress marks to show how Shakespeare most likely pronounced the words.

DUKE ORSINO

If music be the food of love, play on.
Give me excéss of it, that, súrfeiting,
The appetite may sicken and so die.
That strain again! It had a dying fall.
O, it came o'er my ear like the sweet sound
That breathes upon a bank of violets,
Stealing and giving odour. Enough; no more.
'Tis not so sweet now as it was before.
O spirit of love, how quick and fresh art thou!
That, notwithstanding thy capacity
Receiveth as the sea, nought enters there,
Of what validity and pitch soé'er,
But falls into abatement and low price,
Even in a minute. So full of shapes is fancy
That it alone is high fantastical.

Appendix 2: Facts About *Macbeth*

Shakespeare's 29th play (or so)

No record of the first performance
but perhaps August, 1606.

First published in 1623.

Less than 10% prose.
1,560 blank verse lines, including 97 short lines, 35
long lines, and 78 epic caesuras (according to *Shakespeare's*
Metrical Art by George T. Wright)

3 songs (2 heard offstage)

41 characters with lines
7 female speaking parts

The Internet Movie Database lists dozens of filmed
or televised versions of *Macbeth*, including films directed
by Orson Welles and Roman Polanski. The televised version (1979) with Judi Dench and Ian McKellan is widely
praised. Two notable adaptations not using Shakespeare's
dialogue are Akira Kurosawa's *Throne of Blood* (1957) and
Joe Macbeth (1955), a noir gangster film.

Musical adaptations include:
Operas by Guiseppe Verdi (1847), Ernest Bloch (1910),
and Dmitri Shostakovich (1934); a tone poem
by Richard Strauss (1890).

Continuity problems?
In Act 1, Scene 3 Macbeth seems unaware that he has
defeated the treasonous Thane of Cawdor in close combat.
Samuel Johnson felt that this is unlikely.
In Act 3, Scene 6, Lennox and a Lord seem to be dis-

cussing Macbeth's reaction to word that Macduff has gone to England. In Act 4, Scene 1 Lennox first breaks this news to Macbeth. Were the scenes in the wrong order? Could Macbeth have already made preparations for war between the previous night's banquet and his visit to the witches? Perhaps Macbeth alerted his forces in anticipation of Macduff rebuffing him without knowing that Macduff had already fled to England.

Story Credit

Raphael Holinshed's *Chronicles of England, Scotland, and Ireland, 2nd Edition* (1587). Shakespeare's Macbeth combines the actions of a character called Donwald, who conspires with his wife to kill King Duff, and Macbeth, who conspires with Banquo, to kill a weak King Duncan when he exceeds his authority by declaring his son heir to the throne. Holinshed has Macbeth ruling competently for a decade before becoming a despot. In Shakespeare's version, Banquo is innocent of any rebellion, and Macbeth and his wife become tyrants as soon as they gain power.

Sources

Editions of the Plays

The Arden Edition. 1997. Kenneth Muir. London: Thomson Learning.

Bantam Shakespeare. 1988. David Bevington, ed. New York: Bantam Books.

Complete Works (The RSC Shakespeare). 2007. Jonathan Bate and Eric Rasmussen, eds. New York: The Modern Library.

The Everyman Shakespeare. 1990. John F. Andrews, ed. London: J.M. Dent.

The Kittredge Shakespeare. 1967. George Lyman Kittredge, ed/ revised by Irving Ribner. Lexington, Massachusetts:Xerox College Publishing.

The New Cambridge Shakespeare. 1997. A.R. Braunmuller, ed. Cambridge: Cambridge University Press.

The New Folger Library Shakespeare. 1992. Barbara A. Mowat and Paul Werstine, eds. New York: Washington Square Press.

The New Penguin Shakespeare. 1995. G. K Hunter, ed. London: Penguin Books.

The New Variorum Shakespeare. 1963. Horace Howard Furness, ed. New York: Dover Publications. (First published in 1873).

A Norton Critical Edition. 2004. Robert S. Miola, ed. New York and London: W. W. Norton & Company.

The Norton Shakespeare: Based on the Oxford Edition, 2ND Edition. 2008. Stephen Greenblatt, general editor. New York and London: W.W. Norton and Company.

The Pelican Shakespeare. 2000. Stephen Orgell, ed. New York: Penguin Books.

The Oxford Shakespeare. 1990. Nicholas Brooke, ed. Oxford: Oxford University Press.

The Riverside Shakespeare. 1997. Boston and New York: Houghton Mifflin Company.

Shakespeare: Major Plays and the Sonnets. 1948. G. B. Harrison, ed. New York: Harcourt, Brace and World, Inc.

Shakespeare's Tragedy of Macbeth. 1881. William J. Rolfe, A.M., ed. New York: Harper and Brothers, Publishers.

Other Sources

Abbott, E. A. *A Shakespearian Grammar: An Attempt to Illustrate Some Differences Between Elizabethan and Modern English.* 2003. Mineola, New York: Dover Publications, Inc.

Crystal, David and Ben Crystal. *Shakespeare's Words: A Glossary and Language Companion.* 2002. London: Penguin Books.

Compact Edition of the Oxford English Dictionary. 1971. Oxford University Press.

Onions, C.T. *A Shakespeare Glossary.* 1986. Revised and enlarged by Robert D. Eagleson.

Schmidt, Alexander. 1971. *Shakespeare Lexicon and Quotation Dictionary, Volumes 1 and 2.* New York: Dover Publications.

MACBETH

"Leave all the rest to me."

ENJOY SHAKESPEARE

King Lear
Macbeth
Much Ado About Nothing
Romeo and Juliet
Twelfth Night

Check for new titles at
www.FullMeasurePress.com